Quakers and Literature

Quakers and the Disciplines:
Volume 3

Edited by:
James W. Hood

Quakers
and the
Disciplines

Full Media Services
http://www.fullmediaservices.com

Friends Association for Higher Education
http://www.quakerfahe.org

Volume 1.
Quaker Perspectives in Higher Education
May 2014

Volume 2.
Befriending Truth: Quaker Perspectives
June 2015

Volume 3.
Quakers and Literature
June 2016

Volume 4.
2017

Longmeadow, MA | Philadelphia, PA | Windsor, CT

ISBN: 0-9960033-8-X
ISBN-13: 978-0-9960033-8-4

As a venture of the Friends Association for Higher Education, the Quakers and the Disciplines series gathers collections of essays featuring the contributions of Quakers to one or more of the academic disciplines. Noting historic values embraced within the Religious Society of Friends regarding particular fields of inquiry, each volume includes essays highlighting contributions by Quakers as means of addressing the needs of contemporary society. Each volume is designed to be serviceable within classroom and other discussion settings, fostering explorations of how pressing issues of the day might be addressed with creativity and passionate concern, informed by a rich heritage of faith, discovery, and action.

For Jeff, compagnon de voyage

CONTENTS

VOLUME 3: QUAKERS AND LITERATURE

ABOUT THE AUTHORS

J. Ashley Foster is Visiting Assistant Professor of Writing and Fellow in the Writing Program at Haverford College. She defended her dissertation, *Modernism's Impossible Witness: Peace Testimonies from the Modernist Wars*, in May 2014, under the guidance of Jane Marcus. Her articles have been published in *Virginia Woolf Writing the World*, *Virginia Woolf & 20th Century Women Writers*, the *Virginia Woolf Miscellany*, the *Virginia Woolf Bulletin*, and *Interdisciplinary/Multidisciplinary Woolf*. "Stopped at the Border" has been reprinted in Adbusters magazine. Ashley and the students from her spring and fall 2015 "Peace Testimonies in Literature & Art" Writing Seminar curated the interactive student digital humanities and Special Collections exhibition *Testimonies in Art & Action: Igniting Pacifism in the Face of Total War*. This exhibition, which ran in Haverford College's Magill Library from October 6-December 11, 2015, explores pacifism, social justice, and the relationship between art and activism in the interwar era. Ashley's work examines the intersections between pacifism, modernism, and war, and tries to recuperate the lost threads of modernism's pacifist history.

Darlene Graves holds a doctorate in Post-Secondary Educational Leadership and has taught at five universities, including 15 years as director of the drama program at George Fox University in Oregon and 17 years as Artist in Residence at Regent University in Virginia. She has edited and performed in numerous readers theatres, directed 50 theatre productions, produced and toured with more than a dozen theatre ensembles. Her written research and professional presentations focus on the Creative Process, Experiential Learning, and the exploration of the expressive arts as they serve and impact Friends and Faith communities. Darlene is currently a Scholar at Large and resides with her husband, Michael, in Ventura County on the Central Coast of California.

Mike Heller is a Professor of English at Roanoke College where he teaches spiritual autobiography and nonfiction writing, as well as courses in Peace and Justice Studies. He edited *The Tendering Presence: Essays on John Woolman* (Pendle Hill Publications), co-edited a source book on John Woolman (in its 2nd edition) and another on Mohandas K. Gandhi, and has written articles on teaching literature and writing. He is a member of the Roanoke Quaker Meeting. He and his wife, Rebecca A. Heller, live in Roanoke, Virginia, not far from their children and grandchildren.

Ed Higgins is a Professor Emeritus of Writing and Literature at George Fox University in Newberg, Oregon where he has taught for over forty years, and still teaches part-time. His teaching specialties and scholarly interests include fiction writing, ancient world literature, science fiction, Quaker journals, and the contemporary novel. He is also a widely published poet and short fiction writer as well as a part-time organic farmer who draws much of his writing inspiration from his back-to-the-land experiences. His PhD is in early American Quaker Journals. He is a long time member of Friends Association for Higher Education, having served on the Executive Committee from 1988-91.

James W. Hood is Professor of English at Guilford College in Greensboro, North Carolina, where he teaches courses in Romantic and Victorian British literature, literature and ethics, American nature writing, composition, and the natural history of central North Carolina. His publications include works on Alfred Tennyson, John Keats, gothic fiction, and Victorian gift books, and he regularly reviews books for *Friends Journal*. A member of Friendship Friends Meeting (North Carolina Yearly Meeting—Conservative), he has served on the Friends Association for Higher Education executive committee and as clerk of the New Garden Friends School board of trustees.

Marva Hoopes, EdD, serves on the faculty at Malone University in Canton, Ohio as Christian Education Specialist, teaching courses in educational ministry and theology. She has also held positions of Missions Pastor and Children's Pastor for 26 years in the Evangelical Friends Church – Eastern Region. Marva is married to Clark Hoopes and enjoys time with their three adult children and four grandchildren.

William Jolliff is Professor of English at George Fox University. He grew up under the nurture of Fulton Creek Friends Church in Ohio, and currently attends North Valley Friends in Newberg, Oregon, where he serves as facilitator for the unprogrammed meeting. Bill has published hundreds of poems, songs, articles and reviews in a variety of literary journals, and he edited and introduced *The Poems of John Greenleaf Whittier: A Readers' Edition* (Friends United Press, 2000). His most recent collection of original poetry is *Twisted Shapes of Light* (Cascade-Poiema Poetry Series, 2015).

Jon Kershner is adjunct Professor of Theology at Barclay College, Honorary Researcher at Lancaster University (UK), and Tutor at Woodbrooke Quaker Studies Centre (UK). His primary research interests are John Woolman and Global Quakerism. He has written articles on Woolman for *Quaker History*, *Quaker Studies*, *Quaker Religious Thought*, and has a chapter on Woolman in *Quakers and their Allies in the Abolitionist Cause, 1754-1808*. He serves as co-clerk of the Quaker Studies Group at the American Academy of Religion and as co-clerk of the History of Christianity/North American Religions Section of the Pacific Northwest Region of the American Academy of Religion. He is also a Quaker minister in Northwest Yearly Meeting of Friends Churches.

Jean Mulhern recently retired as director of S. Arthur Watson Library, Wilmington College (Ohio), with 10 years of service and 23 years as library director at Wilberforce University. At Wilmington she worked with Dr. T. Canby Jones to organize and preserve his papers and with Dr. D. Neil Snarr to preserve digitally Quaker historical documents held in private collections. She received her Ph.D. in Leadership in Higher Education from the University of Dayton with previous degrees from Kent State University and Heidelberg University (OH). She continues to be active in historical and genealogical research and as a library consultant.

Cathy Pitzer recently retired from Wilmington College (Ohio), where she taught sociology. During her eighteen years of teaching, she designed many innovative projects to encourage students to engage with their local communities in courses such as Society and Business and Rural Sociology. She holds degrees from the University of Pennsylvania and Emory University and is on the Executive Board of the Friends Association for Higher Education. She is currently an agricultural researcher for the U.S. Department of Agriculture in southwest Ohio. She also studies Spanish, golfs, and continues her interests in research and reading mystery novels.

At the 2005 FAHE Conference, **Helene Pollock** had a life-changing spiritual awakening that led her to early Friends. Since then she has been developing programs that help people connect with earlier generations of Friends. She lives in Philadelphia, where she participates in two new Quaker groups and a Black Baptist Church. She maintains connections with Illinois Yearly Meeting, Friends United Meeting and Conservative Friends. In 2009 she retired as Director of Quaker Affairs at Haverford College after eighteen years' service. She holds a B.A. in Spanish from Beloit College, an M.S. in Education from the University of Pennsylvania and an M.Div. from Union Theological Seminary.

Diane Reynolds is adjunct Professor of English at Ohio University Eastern and has a biography of Dietrich Bonhoeffer coming out in winter 2016. She is a member of Ohio Yearly Meeting Conservative, where she serves on M&O and the Friends House Committee.

✳ 1 | Introduction ✳

by James W. Hood

In a brief article entitled "Novel Reading and Insanity" published in Twelfth Month, 1864, the *Friends Intelligencer* leant its imprimatur to a report by Dr. Ray, of the Butler Insane Asylum in Providence, that "light reading" was to blame for the increase of insanity at the present time. "Generally speaking," the *Intelligencer* claimed, "there can be no question that incessant indulgence in novel reading necessarily enervates the mind and diminishes its power of endurance" (611). Echoing what had been a more widespread cultural nervousness about "horrid novels" nearly seventy years earlier, the *Intelligencer* voiced what by that point in time had become a concern about imaginative literature peculiar to stricter religious groups like Quakers:

> In novel reading . . . the mind passively contemplates the scenes that are brought before it, and which, being chiefly addressed to the passions and emotions, naturally please without the necessity of effort or preparation. Of late years a class of books has arisen, the sole object of which is to stir the feelings, not by ingenious plots, not by touching the finer chords of the heart and skillfully unfolding the springs of action, not by arousing our sympathies for unadulterated, unsophisticated goodness, truth and beauty, but by coarse exaggerations of every sentiment, by investing every scene in glaring colors and, in short, by every possible form of unnatural excitement. ... The sickly sentimentality which craves this kind of stimulus is as different from the sensibility of a well-ordered mind as the crimson flush of disease from the ruddy glow of high health. (612)

The fastidious proscription against novel reading expressed here, in a very Quakerly manner that emphasizes the benefits of "a well-ordered mind" and "effort or preparation," provides a mid-nineteenth-century version of the long-standing prohibition in the Religious Society of Friends against indulgence in the various arts. Any discussion of Quakers and literature must almost of necessity begin with an acknowledgement that Friends have only relatively recently embraced creative writing and the arts in general (music, painting, and theater) as a good. For the majority of the Society's existence, Quakers regularly denigrated the arts as at best frivolous and at worst morally depraved. Quaker historical sources remind us that seventeenth-century Friends saw the high arts "as serving the purposes of either the apostate church or the decadent aristocracy" as well as "carnal and self-intoxicating." "Indulgence in sensory gratification, 'vain imaginings,' and useless ornamentation were distractions from attending to the pure Life" and telling stories that never happened was considered untruthful (Abbott et al. 11). Pink Dandelion lists "avoidance of the arts, literature, and anything that was fictional or might excite the natural emotions" (101) as a particular Quaker custom in the Quietist period of the eighteenth century. In a much more limited way, Friends today still eschew artistic expression in some forms, particularly in worship. Even to this day, unprogrammed meetings tend to keep pianos outside the meeting room, and although forms of worship among some Friends altered radically with the advent of paid ministry and programmed meetings in the late nineteenth century, the relative plainness of even contemporary Quaker church sanctuaries testifies to a lingering sense that representations falsify the truth.

Some fundamental friction seems to lie between the Quaker testimonies of simplicity and integrity and the metaphoric, imaginative, carnivalesque spirit that so deeply informs artistic expression. A certain Quaker earnestness, a determined seriousness at the very center of Friends' conceptions of the life turned round right, both in terms of spiritual centeredness and appropriate action in the world, has animated the Society since its inception, and such striving is bound to steer committed Quakers away from pursuits deemed less worthy or necessary. Such incompatibility has also led various creators to abandon the Quakerism into which they were born, finding in themselves too much tension between an artistic calling and the admonitions of Quaker plainness. Stories abound of Quakers who became artists or writers and left the Society or altered their writing upon becoming Quaker. Benjamin West (1738-1820), the British painter, and Charles Brockden Brown (1771-1810), considered the first American novelist, both retreated from membership in the Society of Friends (Abbott et al. 11). Amelia Opie (1769-1853), the British poet, was raised as a Unitarian but became a Quaker after developing a close relationship and correspondence with Joseph John Gurney. As her relationship with Gurney developed, she wrote less and turned more to devotional and didactic poetry, giving up the fiction writing that she had also pursued earlier in her career (Cloyd 20-21). One of the essays in this collection focuses on Rex Stout (1886-1975), the popular twentieth-century American mystery writer who was a birthright Friend and a conscientious objector in World War I, but did not attend meeting and was likely an agnostic, although Quakerism seems to have been a guiding influence throughout his life.

Quakers utilized the power of print assiduously to spread their religious doctrines widely, a fact well chronicled by historians like Kate Peters, but they clearly eschewed writing in the imaginative literary genres. In fact, the Quaker prohibition against artistic endeavor as worldly, false, and frivolous might even be seen as a founding principle of the Society; its presence in Fox's, Penn's, and Barclay's writings suggest it as a bedrock premise. For Fox, writing in *Gospel Truth Demonstrated*, in the section of the book called "A Hammer, To break down all Invented Images, Image-makers, and Image-worshippers. Showing how contrary they are both to the Law and Gospel" (366), the central problem lies in the base falsity of representation itself, the substitution of one thing for another, as well as human beings usurping the role of the Creator:

And therefore, all friends and people, pluck down your images, your likenesses, your pictures, and your representation of things in heaven, things in the earth, and things in the waters; I say, pluck them out of your houses, walls, and signs, or other places, that none of you be found imitators of his Creator, whom you should serve and worship; and not observe the idle lazy mind, that would go invent and make things like a Creator and Maker, any thing (I say) that is in heaven, the earth, or in the waters above or below. (367)

Barclay, when outlining the meaning of integrity in "Proposition 15 – Vain and Empty Customs and Pursuits," notes that "[t]he chief purpose of all religion is to redeem men from the spirit and vain pursuits of this world, and to lead them into inward communion with God," and he condemns all artistic and other endeavors and the pleasures they produce that are not directed toward spiritual development:

Theatrical productions which are not beneficial, frivolous recreation, sports and games which waste precious time and divert the mind from the witness of God in the heart, should be given up. Christians should have a living sense of reverence for God, and should be leavened with the evangelical Spirit which leads into sobriety, gravity, and godly fear. (389)

Frederick Tolles, the twentieth-century literary scholar, in an article outlining ideas about Quaker aesthetics, notes how this well-known statement by William Penn from *No Cross No Crown*—"How many plays did Jesus Christ and his apostles recreate themselves at? What poets, romances, comedies, and the like did the apostles and saints make or use to pass away their time withal?" (qtd. in Tolles 489-90)—"put an end to discussion" about the value of imaginative literature for Quakers (489).

Given the powerful, foundational nature of the Quaker prohibition against the arts and imaginative literature, as well as its lengthy endurance, one might rightly wonder why bother producing a volume of essays about Quakers and literature. What might we hope to gain in pondering the relationship between Friends and creative written expression? The potential pitfalls here are multiple. Such a collection as this could have included a sycophantic paean to John Greenleaf Whittier, who solved the problem of being a Quaker and a poet by writing doctrinally-sound, religious poetry; an overly-reverent survey of do-gooder Quaker characters in fiction, who lack depth and development, especially in nineteenth-century novels and tales, where they were used designedly to promote model behavior and social justice[1]; or a precious accounting of more recent fiction written by Quakers about Quakers, the value of which seems to lie in the facts of their Friendly genesis and content alone. There may well be a time and a place for Quaker self-congratulation, and a volume of essays that celebrates mere Quaker distinctiveness might hold the same place that messages lauding our Friendly quirks have in our meetings for worship. But the scholarly work seen here pushes beyond that into critical analysis and reflection, interrogating historical evidence and even asking, as Diane Reynolds does in her essay, "What could create a Quaker literature as powerful as the best Quaker expository prose and why is this important?"

The relatively recent appearance of two important anthologies of Quaker writing—*Imagination and Spirit: A Contemporary Quaker Reader* (2002), edited by J.

---

[1] James Emmett Ryan examines the way Quaker characters in American fiction were themselves quite fictional, representations utilized to promote particular social or political agendas.

Brent Bill, and *Gathered: Contemporary Quaker Poets* (2013), edited by Nick McRae—suggests that imaginative writing written by openly Quaker Quakers for a larger-than-Quaker audience may be gaining traction. Our literature may be emerging from its very own Quietist period, a first 350 years during which we either wrote mainly for ourselves or had to break away from the Society to write for the greater public. Perhaps "Quaker writer" may be in the formative stages of gaining the kind of meaning that "Catholic writer" has come to possess. Although this volume does not explore that issue in depth, its very presence may suggest the genesis of a new understanding of what it means to be fully Quaker and fully writer simultaneously.

Although this volume covers new ground in the scholarship of Quakers and imaginative literature, it is important to acknowledge earlier scholars who addressed similar issues. For those interested in Quaker characters in fiction of all sorts, Anna Breiner Caulfield's annotated bibliography is an important point of reference. Luella M. Wright's explorations of early Quaker writing may be the first to classify such texts as "literature," though her use of the term differs from its main understanding here. She surveys such genres as the literature of sufferings; essays; allegories and verse; sermons, proverbs, and advices; journals; autobiographies; and religious confessions. This volume treats some texts that fall into such categories, but the bulk of the essays here understand literature in the more limited sense of imaginative, fictional texts (drama, poetry, novels and stories). Dorothy Gilbert Thorne's Ward Lecture in 1959 noted an "increasing interest in the arts" among Friends—more in England than in the United States—and she goes on "to consider the principles which Quakerism and fiction have in common" (3) and to examine how the testimonies and practices of the Society have found their way into fiction and poetry.[2] Howard Hintz's examination of the Quaker presence in American literature, organized by author, traces the Quaker influences in the writings of people like William Penn, Thomas Paine, Charles Brockden Brown, Walt Whitman, and John Greenleaf Whittier, excluding texts that were written by Quakers for Quakers, what he calls "writing which deals directly and specifically with Quakers or Quakerism" (6). He includes under the term "literature" "historical and critical writing as well as fiction, poetry, and other forms of so-called creative writing or *belles lettres*" (6). Though his scholarly interests were broader than literary study exclusively, Frederick B. Tolles

---

[2] Thorne summarizes Ruth Suckow's "four principles" that Quakerism and fiction share: "singlemindedness," the "quality of perceiving ethical and spiritual principle in the abstract, along with a fearless facing and accurate rendering of the mixed world of actuality," "reverence for life," and "care for human life" (6-7).

published on Emerson and Quakerism. More recently in an anthology about literature and ethics, Barbara Heavilin outlines how Quaker religious ideas about love and attention influenced the American ideal of liberty as well as how various Quaker testimonies inform well-known literary texts, such as the call for peace in Wilfred Owen's "Dulce et Decorum Est" and sympathy for the natural environment in William Wordsworth and Gerard Manley Hopkins.

These studies provide important examinations of Quakerism in relation to literature, but they are not many in number, and few of these are recent. The scholarship on Quakerism and literature is not extensive, and this collection aims to fill a gap in the analysis of that relationship. To that end, here readers will find a number of engaging explorations, including J. Ashley Foster's in-depth historical examination of the links between British Modernism, pacifist movements, the Society of Friends, and relief work during the Spanish Civil War. Following in the strong tradition of Quaker scholarly engagement with ethics, Foster's essay analyzes how Virginia Woolf's fictional "Society of Outsiders" in *Three Guineas* had a real-life counterpart in the positive peace efforts developed around the Spanish Civil War and the Aid Spain movement, noting how both of these fictional and actual groups manifest an "intimate ethics" as articulated by Jessica Berman.

The articles about crime novelist Rex Stout, by Cathy Pitzer and Jean Mulhern, and science fiction writer Joan Slonczewski, by Edward F. Higgins, examine the range of relationship between Quakerism and imaginative writing in two very popular genres. Pitzer and Mulhern pose the question of whether Stout, a widely-read mid-twentieth-century crime author born to Quaker parents and raised in Indiana, can be considered a "Quaker author," based on his political leanings, the alignment between his writings and some Quaker testimonies, and his claim, late in life, that he still thought of himself as a Quaker. The genre in which he wrote and his changing attitude towards war— he was a conscientious objector in WWI but advocated early American entry into WWII—make for an engaging consideration of the "Quaker author" question. Higgins' article reads Slonczewski's second novel, *A Door Into Ocean*, very closely, demonstrating fascinating ties between its exploration of feminist utopian society and Quaker ideology. In particular, Higgins examines the significance of links between the women of Shora in the novel and early practitioners of Quakerism.

As one might imagine, John Woolman makes important appearances in this volume, first of all in Jon Kershner's assessment of his relationship to the prophetic tradition, especially Jeremiah who, like Woolman, was reluctant to shoulder the burden of his calling. Tracing the contours of Woolman's "singularity" in relation to his prophetic message, Kershner also takes note of the challenges Woolman's ministry presented to his own faith group and the implications of his ministry for today. Woolman also appears briefly in Helene Pollock's reading of Mary Neale's eighteenth-century memoir. Pollock surveys Neale's life and writing, carefully scrutinizing her understanding of God's power at work in the world and noting differences between her approach and Woolman's. Pollock's explication of Neale's notion of "close work" presents an especially rich account of the difficulty of challenging others and calling them to rely upon the better angels of their nature.

Marva L. Hoopes' contribution explores the power of story itself, particularly in the religious education context, by providing an in-depth look at the amazing accounts in Susanna Morris's (1682-1755) journal of her own "moving accidents" and "hair-breadth scapes" (to borrow phrases from *Othello*) during her work as a Quaker minister. Morris's travels in the ministry over many years included multiple voyages from Pennsylvania, to which she came with her family in 1701, back to England and other parts of Europe. Her journal recounts arduous passages over the Atlantic, shipwrecks, and near-encounters with pirates, all of her "more than common deliverances," as she puts it, from which are signs of God's wondrous providence. Such stories, Hoopes argues, have a transformative power that operates on many "domains of human learning."

Diane Reynolds' essay, as noted earlier, poses a challenge to the community of Friends, asking what it would take to fashion a Quaker imaginative literature as rich and potent as the streams of expository prose for which Friends have long been well known. Working, like Foster, from an ethical theoretical perspective, Reynold's essay takes to task the self-aggrandizing sanctimony too often found in so-called Quaker fiction, offering the example of Helen Morgan Brooks' poetry as an antidote to in-group, Quaker-worshipping pablum.

Historically, poetry was more likely to find acceptance among Friendly readers than fiction. That may have in part been the case because nineteenth-century readers, as William Jolliff demonstrates in his article, more willingly embraced poetry as a means of general communication than we seem to now, heirs that we are to Modernism's turn toward greater difficulty and obscurity in verse. Jolliff raises keen questions about the place of poetry in contemporary culture as he probes what ought to be the role of the Quaker poet in community. His queries regarding the relationship between high art—the poetry of the coterie—and poetry that communicates its meaning(s) more straightforwardly challenge readers to careful consideration of the place imaginative literature need take in our society.

Two other essays, focusing more on pedagogical practice, round out the volume. Darlene Graves surveys the history of Friends' attitudes toward the theatre before exploring ways in which Quaker principles inform both theatre as an academic discipline and the dramatic process. She carefully examines the connections between Quaker spiritual practice and the work of a theatre director, looking in most detail at the practices of the Quaker British theatre group, *The Leaveners*. Mike Heller's piece focuses on an experience teaching a particular course entitled "Nonviolence as a Spiritual Journey." In his essay, Heller recounts taking his students through readings of John Woolman's *Journal*, Mohandas K. Gandhi's *Autobiography*, Dorothy Day's *The Long Loneliness*, and Marian Wright Edelman's *Lanterns: A Memoir of Mentors* as a means of learning about these social activists' lives and allowing the students to reflect in serious fashion about their own struggles of becoming. Heller's essay explores an approach to teaching that asks students, as in Quaker unprogrammed worship, to value their own experience inwardly and outwardly. Students are asked to see their reading and writing as an opportunity to think about knowing "experientially," to look for that which speaks to their condition, and "to let their lives speak."

Since its beginning, imaginative literature has played a critical didactic function in human society, teaching succeeding generations the whims of fate, how one ought to act toward others, and how to shape words into the best prose or poetry. Though in our post-modern condition we may be more reluctant to make bold claims about the instructive value of literature, the essays here remind us that well-imagined texts, through their revelations of human triumphs and foibles, still have an important part to play on the stage of human development. And with our abiding concern for integrity and the equitable treatment of others and our environment, Quakers may have a particular—and if somewhat peculiar, so be it—vantage point from which to examine the ethical and cultural functions of fictional texts. The essays in this volume make abundantly clear the ongoing need for Quaker evaluations of this critical human endeavor.

✳ Works Cited ✳

Abbott, Margery Post, Mary Ellen Chijioke, Pink Dandelion, and John William Oliver, Jr., eds. *Historical Dictionary of the Friends (Quakers)*. *Historical Dictionaries of Religions, Philosophies, and Movements, No. 44*. Lanham, MD and Oxford: Scarecrow Press, 2003. Print.

Barclay, Robert. *Barclay's Apology in Modern English*. Dean Freiday, ed. Manasquan, NJ: Dean Freiday, 1967. Print.

Bill, J. Brent, ed. *Imagination and Spirit: A Contemporary Quaker Reader*. Richmond, IN: Friends United Press, 2002. Print.

Caulfield, Anna Breiner. *Quakers in Fiction: An Annotated Bibliography*. Northampton, MA: Pittenbruach Press, 1993. Print.

Cloyd, Charlotte Langford. "Literary and Religious Manifestations of the Divine: Examining the Intersection between Quakerism and William Wordsworth's Romantic Poems." AB thesis. Guilford College, 2013. Print.

Dandelion, Pink. "Guarded Domesticity and Engagement with 'The World': The Separate Spheres of Quaker Quietism." *Common Knowledge* 16.1 (Dec. 2010): 95-109. *MLA International Bibliography*. 22 June 2015. Web.

Fox, George. *Gospel Truth Demonstrated, in a Collection of Doctrinal Books, Given Forth by that Faithful Minister of Jesus Christ, George Fox: Containing Principles Essential to Christianity and Salvation, Held Among the People Called Quakers*. 1706. Philadelphia: Marcus T.C. Gould; New York: Isaac T. Hopper, 1831. *The Works of George Fox* vol. 4. *Books.google*. 7 July 2015. Web.

Heavilin, Barbara A. "Something to Measure By: Quaker Values in Literature." *Ethics, Literature, Theory: An Introductory Reader*. Lanham, MD: Rowman & Littlefield, 2005. 189-195. Print.

Hintz, Howard W. *The Quaker Influence in American Literature*. New York, NY: Fleming H. Revell, 1940. Print.

McRae, Nick, ed. *Gathered: Contemporary Quaker Poets*. Sundress Publications, 2013. Print.

"Novel Reading and Insanity." *Friends Intelligencer* 21.39 (Twelfth Month 3, 1864): 611-12. *Books.google.com*. Web. 19 June 2015.

Peters, Kate. *Print Culture and the Early Quakers*. Cambridge, UK; New York: Cambridge University Press, 2005. Print.

Ryan, James Emmett. "Imaginary Friends: Representing Quakers in Early American Fiction." *Studies in American Fiction* 31.2 (2003): 191-220. *MLA International Bibliography*. Web. 22 June 2015.

Thorne, Dorothy Gilbert. *Quakerism in Fiction and Poetry Recently Written by Women*. Tenth Annual Ward Lecture. Guilford College, 6 Nov. 1959. Print.

Tolles, Frederick B. "'Of the Best Sort but Plain': The Quaker Esthetic." *American Quarterly* 11.4 (Winter 1959): 484-502. *JSTOR*. 22 June 2015. Web.

---. "Emerson and Quakerism." *American Literature: A Journal of Literary History, Criticism, and Bibliography* 10.2 (1938): 142-165. *MLA International Bibliography*. Web. 14 July 2015.

Wright, Luella M. *The Literary Life of the Early Friends, 1650-1725*. New York: Columbia UP, 1932. Print.

---. *Literature and Education in Early Quakerism*. Iowa City, IA: 1932. Print.

✳2| Quaker Spiritual Literature ✳

"Diminish Not a Word":
The Prophetic Voice of John Woolman

by Jon R. Kershner

Introduction

The theme of the 2015 Friends Association for Higher Education gathering was "Truth and Transformation," and that theme got me thinking about prophets (biblical and otherwise), the prophetic vocation, and my dear friend John Woolman (1720-1772).

John Woolman is one of the most famous of American Quakers. For some, including myself, the story of Woolman was a door into Quakerism.

Woolman was born in 1720 near Mount Holly, New Jersey. He was raised in a devout Quaker family. As a young man, he left the family farm and apprenticed in a retail shop where he learned to keep books, manage a store, and the skills of a tailor. In his early twenties, he felt that he was called to a life of greater spiritual depth, but he struggled to give up the life he said was characterized by "youthful vanities" and "mirth" (Woolman, "Journal" 26). It wasn't easy for Woolman to respond obediently to God's call. He struggled. He described in his *Journal* feelings of hopelessness and shame when he slipped back into his old ways. And he described those tastes of joy and promise he experienced whenever he took a step forward in his spiritual life.

Woolman's spiritual awakening in his early twenties coincided with his experience of being called to ministry. He wrote in his *Journal*, "From one month to another [I felt] love and tenderness [increase], and my mind was more strongly engaged for the good of my fellow creatures, [and I found it too strong… to be much longer confined to my own breast]" (Woolman, "Journal" 30).

And a short time later, Woolman experienced a moment of commissioning, a calling that God had appointed him to bear a message, to testify to the ways of God in the world. Woolman wrote, "I felt that rise which prepares the creature to stand like a trumpet through which the Lord speaks to his flock" (Woolman, "Journal" 30).

Woolman was approved as a Quaker minister by his local Quaker meeting in his early twenties and began to travel on ministry journeys up and down the colonies. On average, he spent a month a year on ministry journeys. He travelled south to North Carolina, north into New England, and across the Atlantic to England, where he walked from London to York visiting Quaker meetings along the way. He died of smallpox in York in 1772, at the age of fifty-two.

During his life he worked as a shop-keeper and proprietor of his successful store before curtailing his retail business in order to expand his ministry. He worked as a tailor, he wrote legal documents, he had a farm, grafted fruit trees, and spent some years as a school teacher. He even authored a primer for children to use as they learned to read and write (Woolman, "A First Book for Children").

Woolman is best known as an early antislavery advocate who helped to lead Quakers toward a corporate antislavery position. Woolman did not see the end of Quaker involvement in slavery during his lifetime, but he did see considerable movement toward a corporate antislavery position among Quakers. When he was a young man in Philadelphia Yearly Meeting, slavery was generally accepted by many Quakers. Before 1750, Quaker slave-ownership rates in Philadelphia were about the same as the Philadelphia population as a whole (Marietta 115–116). However, Woolman's reforms went beyond slavery and included criticisms of British economic practices, the abuse of laborers, and war.

Woolman also maintained practices that his peers thought to be extreme. Beginning in his forties, Woolman dressed in undyed clothing as a spiritual sign to the purity and authenticity God wanted all people to embody. He also thought that merchants should only sail their ships when directly led by the Spirit to do so, and not according to the demands of economic interests and wealth accumulation.

The *Journal* is Woolman's spiritual autobiography, which he began writing at the age of thirty-six (Woolman, "Journal" 23). Quaker journal writing was an important tool for teaching others of the spiritual life and followed an

QUAKERS AND THE DISCIPLINES

established form. Not all Quakers wrote journals, and not every journal was published. The aim of journal writers was to show, through the example of their lives, how one was to follow the leadings of the Spirit. The purpose of the journal, then, was didactic, spiritual, and practical (Wright 155). Those Quakers who wrote journals were those who were seen as embodying the best of their religious tradition, and whose example helped to further the religious goals and spiritual longings of the community.

By 1725 there were twenty-five Quaker journals in print and circulating among Woolman and his peers (Wright 156). Quaker journals tended to follow the pattern of tracing the author's spiritual life through stages of youthful rebellion, surrender to God, calling to ministry, and the day to day development of sensitivity to God's leadings. A journal was not the comprehensive history of the author's life, but, rather, was focused on those events that were deemed to be spiritually instructive. Woolman's *Journal* follows the basic template of other Quaker journals, but is original in the degree of eschatological transformation he expected and the integrated way he combined a social and spiritual vision for colonial America (Kershner 297–318; Heller 186).

In addition to the *Journal,* Woolman wrote essays intended to provide a spiritual and theological case for increased attention to the voice of God and for the consequent behavioral changes he thought would ensue. Woolman viewed his writings as extensions of his ministry and part of his faithfulness to God. Taken together, the written record of his ministry depicts for future generations the way his inward spiritual attention and outward embodiment attempted to interpret God's will for his community and to provide a way of navigating faithfully in a complex and changing world.

Praise for Woolman

It is hard to underestimate John Woolman's influence on Western civilization, both in regard to his role in antislavery and in his shaping of a uniquely American spirituality, even though he is largely unknown outside of Quaker circles today.

Fifty years after Woolman's death, the English writer Charles Lamb said "The only American book I ever read twice was the Journal of John Woolman... Get the writings of John Woolman by heart" (Slaughter 4–5).

Samuel Taylor Coleridge said, "I should almost despair of that man who could peruse the life of John Woolman without an amelioration of heart" (Slaughter 5). Coleridge reflected the experience that many readers of Woolman have: reading Woolman sensitizes your heart and soul and increases one's desire to be a better person.

John Greenleaf Whittier credited Woolman with founding the abolitionist movement. And indeed, Woolman's *Journal* influenced the abolitionism of Thomas Clarkson, William Wilberforce, and Tsar Alexander II's emancipation of Russian serfs in 1861 (Moulton 12–14).

Perhaps the highest praise of all came from the proslavery governor of Missouri and confederate army General who, in 1853, unknowingly paid Woolman a compliment when he blamed Woolman personally for the "evils" of the trans-Atlantic abolitionist movement (Slaughter 5).

Willard Sperry, dean of Harvard from 1925-1953 said of Woolman: "If I were asked to date the birth of social conscience in its present-day form, I think I should put it on... the day John Woolman in a public meeting verbally denounced Negro slavery" (Slaughter 5).

More recently, Philips Moulton declared that Woolman "deserves to be ranked among the great spiritual leaders of mankind... comparable to such better known figures as Albert Schweitzer and Mahatma Gandhi" (Slaughter 6).

For some, Woolman's message is one of simplicity, for others it is one of equality and crossing racial and religious boundaries. I've found Woolman to be all of these, of course. But I've mostly found Woolman to be a deeply unsettling presence, the prick in my conscience that will not leave me alone, who challenges the fragmented and secularist way I think about the issues of our day, and that presents me with a vision of a world remade.

What distinguishes Woolman from myself is that I am tempted to use my truth as a bludgeon that is all too happy to create change through intellectual coercion. However, Woolman did not view Truth as something that could be wielded, but as something that consumes one's life and in that experience of being spiritually and holistically consumed leads to comprehensive transformation—a transformation that goes beyond the victory of one opinion over another, but is enraptured in a socio-spiritual revolution that is universal and eternal. In other words, for Woolman, the prophetic vocation was about being subject to something beyond himself, a message that had as its goal the union of God and humanity and the submission of all aspects of human affairs to the direct and inward voice of God. I have found Woolman's prophetic voice to be challenging and unwelcome because in its comprehensiveness it leaves me no place to hide; it rejects the compartmentalized and fragmentary way I create boundaries around the places in my life, and in my heart, that I would rather leave untouched, protected, and hidden.

Woolman the Troublemaker

I am not the first to find Woolman to be a troubling figure. While we often think of Woolman as a luminary, a standout, the most authentic representative of eighteenth century Quakerism, the truth is that, in his own day, he was not esteemed differently from any number of other Quaker ministers. Not only that, many Quakers did not know what to do with him and many found his views and habits excessive.

The Editing of John Woolman

To deal with some of his behaviors, soon after his death, he was edited and tamed. Three years after Woolman's death, in 1775, London Yearly Meeting published an edition of Woolman's *Works* that excised his more unpopular sentiments. Gone were two supernatural visions. Cut out were references to refusing to pay war taxes and his criticisms of the British trans-Atlantic imperial economy. His attacks on low wages, animal abuse, dyed cloth, small pox inoculations, and silver cups were rejected. Some of his antislavery writings were watered down and abridged. The image of Woolman that resulted was of a pious model of lowliness, self-effacement, and humility. John Woolman, meek and mild. A spirituality devoid of moral embodiment and socio-political transformation (Plank 77).

Not all of Woolman's ideas found acceptance during his life. The Philadelphia Yearly Meeting committee tasked with overseeing publications sometimes insisted that he change some of the passages in his essays. A chapter to one of his essays entitled "Serious Considerations on Trade" was not accepted by the committee upon submission and, when Woolman and the committee could not agree on the proposed changes, the chapter was withheld completely (Woolman, *Journal Folio A*). Woolman knew that his writings would be subjected to the editorial knife when he submitted them; it was part of the process of publication. But these editorial changes and rejections suggest that Woolman and his peers had differing opinions on what faithfulness looked like, and that some in Philadelphia Yearly Meeting held at least some ambivalence about Woolman's vision for colonial America.

Singularity

Many of his peers considered Woolman to be "singular." To be "singular" was not a good thing. The label meant that Woolman's views in some areas were not prerequisite to being a good Quaker, and, in some cases, implied that Woolman was dangerously close to stepping outside the bounds of accepted Quaker behavior. When Woolman set sail to England in 1772, unbeknownst to him, his good friend John Pemberton sent a letter in advance of Woolman's arrival recommending him, and warning some key Quakers that Woolman might appear to be a radical on first encounter but that he was, actually, a worthy Friend. "[John Woolman] is a truly upright man," Pemberton wrote, "but walks in a straiter path than some other good folks are led… It will be safest for Friends with you to leave him much to his own feelings, and to walk and steer in that path which proves most easy to him, without using much arguments of persuasion" (Cadbury 52) .

Fellow American Quaker minister, Samuel Emlen, travelled to England with Woolman and in his travels heard of the disapproval Woolman encountered, and wrote home to his wife about it:

> London 5 of 9mo 1772 7th day:
> … thou wilt esteem it prudent to be wholly silent about [the] unacceptance of worthy John Woolman's white dress. To some it is unpleasing, but wisdom and authority are with him in his Gospel labors, and that strongly obviates with me the difficulty of singularity in superficial appearance. (Cadbury 18)

One leading British Quaker was not as generous. He wrote: "John Woolman is solid and weighty in his remarks. I wish he could be cured of some singularitys [sic]. But his real worth outweighs the trash" (Cadbury 6). In this particular letter there is uncertainty whether or not the final word is "trash" or "husk," but, in either case, many Quakers thought some of Woolman's habits were unsupportable and should be discarded.

Perhaps the person most upset by Woolman's "singularity" was Woolman himself. He knew he held different positions from others, he knew that when he walked into town in his undyed clothing, people were making all sorts of assumptions about his motivations, and it caused him emotional turmoil. Some likely thought he was a sell-out to style and fashion, others thought he was an attention-seeker.

It was not just his clothes that made Woolman singular. On one of his ministry journeys Woolman acknowledged that many Quakers, and many of his fellow ministers, did not have the same conviction against slavery that he did. "Though in this thing I appear singular from many whose service in travelling I believe is greater than mine," Woolman wrote, "I do not think hard of them for omitting it. I do not repine at having so unpleasant a task assigned me, but look with awfulness to him who appoints to his servants their respective employments and is good to all who serve him sincerely" (Woolman, "Journal"

108). He wrote that only the inward vindication of obeying God's voice could support someone "to bear patiently the reproaches attending singularity" (Woolman, "Plea for the Poor" 247).

Undyed Clothing

As Woolman adopted the habit of wearing undyed clothes, he knew he was breaking Quaker convention. He was not cavalier or flippant about the witness he felt God ask of him. He felt it to be arduous and knew the reproach he would garner.

He wrote that, "The apprehension of being singular from my beloved friends was a strait upon me, and thus I remained in the use of some things contrary to my judgment" (Woolman, "Journal" 120). Woolman found courage to overcome his uneasiness and anxiety in the conviction that his "singularity" was for the sake of obedience to God and that it was God's authority that enlivened his concern: "the apprehension of being looked upon as one affecting singularity felt uneasy to me," Woolman said. "And here I had occasion to consider that things, though small in themselves, being clearly enjoined by divine authority became great things to us, and I trusted the Lord would support me in the trials that might attend singularity while that singularity was only for his sake" (Woolman, "Journal" 121).

But Woolman was never completely comfortable with the distance that his calling placed between him and his peers, and so he looked to the prophetic commissioning narratives of the Hebrew prophets as encouragement and inspiration. In a passage chock full of Biblical allusions, Woolman wrote:

> The repeated charges which God gave to his prophets imply the danger they were in of [being influenced by human opinion]: 'Be not afraid of their faces; for I am with thee to deliver thee, saith the Lord.' Jer. 1:8. 'Speak... all the words that I command thee to speak to them; diminish not a word.' Jer. 26:2. 'And thou son of man, be not afraid of them... nor dismayed at their looks. Speak my words to them, whether they will bear of forebear.' Ezek. 2:6[-7]. (Woolman, "Considerations on Keeping Negroes" 212)

The distress Woolman felt when he challenged Quaker norms and when he envisioned a world of socio-spiritual "Harmony" that nobody else seemed to want was only mitigated by the intensity of divine revelations that were as real, direct, and understandable to him as if they were given person-to-person. Woolman's experience of God's revelatory presence led him to look for kindred spirits in the Hebrew prophets, and, especially, the prophet Jeremiah.

A Prophet Like Jeremiah

Jeremiah, known as the reluctant prophet, was a model to Woolman of someone who would rather not be a prophet, thank you very much. Jeremiah wanted his message to go away and leave him alone. He wanted to be just like everybody else, he did not want to bear bad news against his neighbors. Like Jeremiah, the revelation of God to Woolman was one that challenged those dilutions of faithfulness and obedience that occur whenever humanity turns its energy into destructive egocentrisms, oppression, and negations of God's creative intent for human thriving. All those corruptions of divine-human intimacy that only lead to spiritual and social alienation.

On one occasion, while traveling in the South, Woolman attended an annual gathering of Quaker ministers and elders in which he felt led by God to confront the group with their sin, though his *Journal* does not identify what that sin was (Woolman, "Journal" 52). Directly after sharing his leading to confront the group, he wrote about the necessity of enduring in the midst of conflict because God's calling could not be resisted:

> Through the humbling dispensations of divine providence men are sometimes fitted for his service. The messages of the prophet Jeremiah were so disagreeable to the people and so reverse to the spirit they lived in that he became the object of their reproach and in the weakness of nature thought to desist from his prophetic office, but saith he: '[God's] word was in my heart as a burning fire shut up in my bones, and I was weary with forbearing and could not stay' [Jer. 20:9]. I saw at this time that if I was honest to declare that which Truth opened in me, I could not please all men, and laboured to be content in the way of my duty, however disagreeable to my own inclination. (Woolman, "Journal" 52)

Nowhere in Woolman's writings does he ever appear giddy to take prophetic stances that he knows would be opposed by his fellow colonists and Quakers. Woolman was not looking for a fight. Like the prophet Jeremiah, he found the message God had given to him a burden, an exercise, a duty, a solemn calling that brought with it interpersonal turmoil and anxiety.

Woolman's genius was that he did not place himself over and above his peers, even in those places where his conviction was strong. Rather, the distance between his sense of God's leading and the apostasy he saw in the world around him caused him grief. He did not lambaste his fellow Quakers for their positions and for the oppressive systems they supported, he grieved for them. On several occasions he was reduced to tears when confronted with hardened hearts, and when he found himself under compunction from God to walk a different path than his acquaintances and friends (Woolman, "Journal" 72, 119). Woolman could not caricature or demean those who felt differently than he on the most controversial issues of his day, because he was committed to his community and he knew that his convictions were not his own invention. Since his vision for human faithfulness was given to him by God, they belonged to God and so it was to God that he entrusted them.

In 1757, Woolman visited yearly meeting sessions in the South and noticed that some antislavery statements had been watered down. Woolman spoke in protest, but the change in language was admitted anyway. Woolman saw that he could not push any further and he said "[I] felt easy to leave all to him who alone is able to turn the hearts of the mighty and make way for the spreading of Truth in the earth by means agreeable to his infinite wisdom" (Woolman, "Journal" 66–67).

Later, on that same journey, Woolman described the type of prophetic non-attachment that invigorated both his obedience to the divine voice and his commitment to Quaker community:

> Travelling up and down of late, I have had renewed evidences that to be faithful to the Lord and content with his will concerning me is a most necessary and useful lesson for me to be learning, looking less at the effects of my labour than at the pure motion and reality of the concern as it arises from heavenly love. (Woolman, "Journal" 72)

For Woolman, the message was authored by God, and, so, held by God. And its fulfillment, too, was in God's hands. Attentiveness to the Source of divine revelation was the litmus test for prophetic authenticity, and by placing his focus on God's voice Woolman embodied the spiritual transformation out of which his social vision arose. Woolman was deeply concerned with the issues of his day: lotteries, high rents and interest rates, poverty, egregious wealth, alcoholism, the rapaciousness of the British trans-Atlantic imperial economy. But he did not merely have a list of issues on which he took public stands, as if they could all be isolated, fragmented, and compartmentalized. Woolman's prophetic voice was a comprehensive and unified whole: Respond to the motion of love, respond to the motion of love, respond to the motion of love. By pointing, again and again, to the spiritual root and cause that taught him what a world remade would look like, Woolman avoided becoming merely a partisan. Like the Hebrew prophets, Woolman saw that the social degeneracies of his day were symptoms of spiritual alienation and rebellion. Woolman's challenge to his fellow colonists was to hearken back to the "pure motion and reality" of God's will.

Outside of a state of obedience within God's will, outside of the complete surrender of one's self to God, slavery happens. Economic and physical bondage happens. Greed happens. While Woolman had many friends and was admired by quite a few, his message was not co-opted by any social or political group within eighteenth-century society. Woolman's letters show that not even his closest friends and allies escaped the unrelenting energy of his commission to call people back, over and over, to the presence of God and to warn them of the pride that put them in eternal jeopardy.

In the spirit of Jeremiah, Woolman was the reluctant prophet. Called to a testimony he did not want, with a message he would have rather ignored. Because he knew that his message was one that originated elsewhere, he could only grieve for those to whom he was sent, and grieve for the path he must walk. But his grief was also his vindication. He took assurance from the fact that his message caused him angst and was contrary to his own inclinations, because that validated for him that his message was not of his own but was from God.

The Prophetic Task

Biblical scholar Walter Brueggemann says that "grief and mourning, that crying in pathos, is the ultimate form of criticism" of the oppressive and spiritually alienating system (Brueggemann 46). Brueggemann suggests that the two elements of Jeremiah's grief were, first, his grief for the people who were approaching their end; and, second, grief because no one would listen and no one saw what was so transparent to him (Brueggemann 47).

Woolman's grief grounded the social manifestations of his calling in love for his people, his friends, and neighbors. It was a love that believed the apathetic, self-centered stagnation that passed for religion among some of his fellow Quakers was too small a thing and too puny a calling for a people sent by God to be in the vanguard of God's will for human destiny. Prophetic ministry brings the claims of the tradition into an effective confrontation with the historical situation of enculturation. The prophet takes the tradition seriously. The prophet is one who has been shaped by the tradition and whose field of perception and system of vocabulary is intricately informed by the tradition. The prophet is so at home in the collective memory of that tradition that, as Brueggeman writes, "the points of contact and incongruity with the situation of the church in culture can be discerned and articulated with proper urgency" (Brueggemann 2).

However, that the prophet is shaped by the tradition does not mean that the prophet does not also live in tension with it. The prophet is one who innovates and reinvigorates that tradition so that it does not fall captive to tribalism, insularity, and accommodation.

G. Thomas Couser has traced the prophetic mode within the American autobiographical tradition, including Woolman's *Journal*. Couser writes that

> the prophet interprets the history of his community in the light of God's will; he speaks, then, for God to his community. But by virtue of this fact, he also functions as a representative of his community - as a reformer of its ethos, articulator of its highest ideals, interpreter of its history, and activist in the service of its best interests. Typically, his stance is one of opposition to the status quo or the apparent flow of history, but he is a critic rather than a schismatic; his ultimate loyalty is to divine principles, but his immediate concern is with the community's destiny. (Couser 3)

Couser identifies Woolman's *Journal* as a prime example of American prophetic autobiography. He writes that:

> Prophetic autobiography flourishes in times of crisis - when change threatens communal values or when historical developments demand new modes of interpretation. It requires of the autobiographer a sense of his implication in the crisis and a theology or metaphysics capable of comprehending it. His presumption that he possesses a vision justifying his prophetic stance is matched by his sense of the community's need for it and perhaps balanced by his recognition that the vision is theirs as much as it is his. (Couser 3)

Woolman stands within a tradition of prophetic spiritualists, dissenters and what I would call apocalyptists. The word "apocalypse" refers to the unveiling of a new world, a revelation of ultimate human fulfillment, of eternity weaving itself into temporality and birthing an alternative socio-spiritual consciousness. Woolman believed that the world of the spirit and the physical world were intertwined and that God was bringing about a new world that repudiated the values, politics, economics, and structures of a world alienated from God and God's purposes.

The prophet delegitimizes and rejects the present ordering of things while fostering and pointing to an alternative consciousness that energizes communities with its promise of another way of being toward which the community may faithfully move (Brueggemann 3). Brueggeman argues, *"The task of prophetic ministry is to nurture, nourish, and evoke a consciousness and perception alternative to the consciousness and perception of the dominant culture around us"*

(Brueggemann 3). Woolman viewed his prophetic commissioning in those terms.

Challenging Tribalism

Woolman was committed to Quakers all the while challenging Quaker tribalism with a vision of the world he thought God was bringing about. When Woolman began wearing undyed clothing in the 1760s, he did it to topple the false religiosity, self-righteousness, and superficiality that allowed Quakers to be esteemed outwardly while their inward state was one of spiritual degeneracy and moral corruption.

While the first generation of Quakers in the 1650s protested the way religious rituals and hierarchies alienated people from a real and direct inward experience of the voice of Christ, Woolman saw that the greed and socio-economic oppression underlying the British imperial economy was every bit as spiritually destructive as the religious controls of a century before. Woolman believed that many Quakers had been enculturated into the colonial, imperial ethos of his day and had reduced the direct and transforming spiritual experience that enlivened the first generation of Friends to a set of tribal behaviors that hid the true corruption of their enculturation. One could don the Quaker garb, attend Meeting for Worship regularly, follow all the rules of Quaker membership, and still be involved in war, slavery, and taking advantage of day laborers; and still reject the spiritual transformation that was at the root of the original Quaker experience.

It is true that plants used to make the dyes that colored eighteenth-century clothes were often harvested by slaves and that the process of creating the dyes was polluting, but these were not the reasons Woolman gave for his decision to wear undyed clothing. Woolman saw the Quaker practice of wearing darkly dyed garments as a metaphor for their spiritual condition. Dyes were a substance applied to clothing that weakened them and whose primary purpose was to create the appearance of cleanliness, to hide the dirt. Like Quaker tribal practices in which prescribed behaviors gave the appearance of faithfulness when the underlying reality was one of spiritual decay, dyed clothing was just a covering for filth meant to provide the appearance of cleanliness (Woolman, "Journal" 190).

Woolman challenged behaviors that had been associated with Quaker faithfulness, but that had lost their rootedness in the spiritually-transforming experience. By wearing undyed clothing, Woolman defied a Quaker practice that had become a hindrance to the spiritual authenticity and transparency that was a requirement for life in the power of God.

The core of Woolman's prophetic voice was his consistent call to return to the experience of spiritual light and life without which Quaker action was nothing more than religious performance. Woolman did not view this calling as one confined to the religious dimensions of one's life and so segmented away from the totality of human experience. Rather, he envisioned an apocalypse of the heart in which the direct spiritual presence of Christ governed human affairs with the perfect fullness of God's will. Woolman attacked those practices and habits that hindered the activity of the Spirit in the world, which oppressed the soul, and that contradicted the divine intent for socio-spiritual harmony. In the apocalypse of the heart, Woolman believed the Spirit of Christ would so transform the individual as to show them an alternative vision of society, a perfected and just ordering that reflected God's ultimate intent for human destiny, but available now, on earth, through human faithfulness. Woolman said of this vision in 1772: "In the harmonious Spirit of Society, Christ is all in all. Here it is *that Old Things are past away, all Things are new, all things are of God;* and the Desire for outward Riches is at an End" (Woolman, "On Loving Our Neighbours as Ourselves" 491–492). The social dimensions of Woolman's prophetic voice found cohesion in a vision of a world made new, where greed and oppressive practices were no longer possible because their root cause was no longer viable in the new world of absolute human dependency on God.

If eighteenth- and nineteenth-century Quakers edited Woolman's writings in ways that diminished the social aspects of his witness it might be that contemporary Quakers tend toward the reduction of his spiritual radicalism.

Implications

In my estimation, Woolman understood himself to be within the prophetic tradition of Jeremiah, Protestant martyrs, and other reformers who were willing to die and endure persecution in obedience to the voice of God they discerned. The politically and socially subversive elements of Woolman's apocalyptic vision, such as his view of Christ literally directing all matters of economy and politics, can be a barrier between Woolman and people of the twenty-first century.

Indeed, the more I know of Woolman the more uncomfortable I am with him, because to take him seriously is to let him question the assumptions I take for granted. Woolman challenges the individualism that preempts true corporate discernment and listening. Woolman exposes the destructiveness of the commodification of people and systems originally intended to serve human thriving. That commodification takes place in the ongoing benefit we take from the nearly 30 million invisible and nameless modern-day slaves who make the clothes on our bodies, and the electronics in our pockets; that commodification looks like an educational system that trumps occupation over vocation, developing quantifiable test-takers over developing conscientious global citizens.

These challenges make it difficult to extrapolate the fullness of Woolman's prophetic voice to the lives of people in the twenty-first century, who live in a very different age with very different ideas about what a rightly ordered world might look like. Like Woolman, we are looking with expectancy for the transformation of what is into consistency with what may be, and like Woolman we hope that what we do now might be a foretaste of the socio-spiritual harmony we desire to become the norm for human walking on the earth.

And perhaps on that front Woolman does provide us some insight. Woolman did not outline a 10-step plan toward implementing his vision; his writings are frustratingly sparse when it comes to the practicalities and logistics of a world remade. I think Woolman encountered this criticism in his own day. On multiple occasions Woolman reiterated the conviction that while he did not know how people could extricate themselves from slavery, the constrictions of wealth, and the pride that underlie it all, he had faith that God would provide a way out. The act of resignation to the divine will, itself, would provide the map for change, redemption, and transformation. Again and again, Woolman held up the prospect that the new world God was establishing on earth was one characterized by an intimate and direct hear-and-obey relationship with humanity, and, again and again, he declared that the path toward the implementation of that vision was to turn, even now, and respond to that Transforming Presence.

Woolman was not merely advocating that people live more simply than they already are, to wit, drive the Honda Civic Hybrid instead of the Honda Civic. He wanted to throw over the existing categories of piety, religious tribalism, and imperial enculturation; he wanted to smash the frame that had bounded Quaker sensibilities; and he wanted to advocate instead the dictatorship of Christ over all aspects of human affairs. His answer to religious tribalism was not secularism, but a dynamic Christocracy that was more radical than the paltry fare of religious accommodation he witnessed around him. He called colonists, and us, to become subjects to the one Voice out of which any voice that is prophetic must spring; to the one thing that upends and redefines all others, and recreates the world with spiritual resources that cannot be boiled down to flow-charts, but that can only be truly known in a life transformed.

Woolman found his prophetic voice in the commissioning he felt could only come from a divine source, directed into human community. What we see in Woolman is that the prophetic voice is not primarily seen in the oppositional positions a person takes but in the community a person builds. A prophetic voice is legitimated by one's advocacy of issues relating to deeper spiritual growth and by the enhancement of the community in which one has been placed. Often this will mean taking the long view, like Woolman did. Woolman, who felt clear to leave "all to [the One] who alone is able to turn the hearts of the mighty and make way for the spreading of Truth," did not see the end of slavery among Quakers in his life. Taking the long view means finding a place to stand and to have a voice, but it opens the door for grace and community and to trust that the work of Truth is ultimately unstoppable, but that it cannot be forced.

The way Woolman has exercised his prophetic voice is a helpful corrective to my own tendency to be strident in those places where I form positions of opposition to my neighbors and colleagues, which I would like to think are prophetic but that have at least some footing in self-righteousness and my own enculturation. While we don't often associate humility with being prophetic, Woolman, and Jeremiah before him, are examples of just that. When the prophetic voice arises from a humble heart, it has the power to build community, preserve dignity, and point to the social and interpersonal harmony that is the vision of the prophetic imagination.

✳ **Works Cited** ✳

Brueggemann, Walter. *The Prophetic Imagination*. 2nd ed. Minneapolis, MN: Fortress Press, 2001. Print.

Cadbury, Henry. *John Woolman in England a Documentary Supplement*. London: Friends Historical Society, 1971. Print.

Couser, G. Thomas. *American Autobiography: The Prophetic Mode*. Amherst, MA: University of Massachusetts Press, 1979. Print.

Heller, Michael. "Soft Persuasion: A Rhetorical Analysis of John Woolman's Essays and Journal." Diss. Arizona State University, 1989. Print.

Kershner, Jon R. "'The Government of Christ': John Woolman's (1720-1772) Apocalyptic Theology." University of Birmingham, 2013. Print.

Marietta, Jack D. *The Reformation of American Quakerism, 1748-1783*. Philadelphia, PA: University of Pennsylvania Press, 1984. Print.

Moulton, Phillips. "Introduction." *The Journal and Major Essays of John Woolman*. Richmond, IN: Friends United Press, 1971. 13. Print.

Plank, Geoffrey. "The First Person in Antislavery Literature: John Woolman, His Clothes and His Journal." *Slavery and Abolition* 30.1 (2009): 67–91. Print.

Slaughter, Thomas P. *The Beautiful Soul of John Woolman, Apostle of Abolition*. New York: Hill and Wang, 2008. Print.

Woolman, John. "A First Book for Children: Much Useful Reading Being Sullied and Torn by Children in Schools Before They Can Read, This Book Is Intended to Save Unnecessary Expense." *John Woolman and the Affairs of Truth: The Journalist's Essays, Epistles, and Ephemera*. Ed. James Proud. San Francisco, CA: Inner Light Books, 2010. 129–145. Print.

---. "A Plea for the Poor, or A Word of Remembrance and Caution to the Rich." *The Journal and Major Essays of John Woolman*. Ed. Phillips P. Moulton. Richmond, IN: Friends United Press, 1971. 238–272. Print.

---. "Considerations on Keeping Negroes; Recommended to the Professors of Christianity of Every Denomination; Part Second." *The Journal and Major Essays of John Woolman*. Ed. Phillips P. Moulton. Richmond, IN: Friends United Press, 1971. 210–237. Print.

---. "Journal." *The Journal and Major Essays of John Woolman*. Ed. Phillips P. Moulton. Richmond, IN: Friends United Press, 1971. 23–192. Print.

---. *Journal Folio A*. Woolman Papers. Historical Society of Pennsylvania. Box 737.

---. "On Loving Our Neighbours as Ourselves." *The Journal and Essays of John Woolman*. Ed. Amelia M. Gummere. New York: Macmillan Company, 1922. 489–496. Print.

Wright, Luella M. *The Literary Life of the Early Friends, 1650-1725,*. New York: Columbia University Press, 1932. Print.

Learning From Mary Neale
(1717-1757)

by Helene Pollock

Mary Neale (*nee* Peisley) was an eighteenth-century Quaker traveling minister and author of a 120-page Quietist memoir of soaring, elegant prose. It is my contention that Mary Neale's primary focus was on the power of God, as she was "spiritually empowered" (my term, not hers) and as she encouraged the Quaker community at a time of widespread complacency. A few of Neale's vignettes are found in the Appendix. These quotations illustrate how she saw the discipline of "humility of mind" (putting self aside) to be integral to her experience of God's power.

As a traveling minister, Mary Neale visited meetings and met with individual Friends, which was a daunting task in every sense. Very often, situations confounded her. Many times she found herself physically ill or beset by deep anguish, which in time she invariably came to view as having been necessary for God's wider purposes. As she waited for divine guidance, sometimes she needed to be entirely passive. At other times she needed to act decisively, for example disengage ("clear herself") from a situation that was clouding her judgment. Each manifestation of God's power invariably filled her with a deep, abiding sense of peace.

This paper includes an overview of Neale's life and writing, followed by a very limited comparison between some aspects of Neale's memoir and the well-known journal of John Woolman (1720-1772). The purpose of this comparison is to get a clearer picture of Neale's particular way of looking at God's power.

In order to make sense of the eighteenth-century worldview that frames these texts, it is necessary to step back from many thought patterns that seem "normal" to us as twenty-first century readers; for example, our emphasis on quantifiable goals and our allegiance to belief systems that promote ever-increasing self-esteem, self-reliance and initiative.

Biographical information about Mary Neale

Mary Neale was raised in humble surroundings in a Quaker community in Ireland. While the Quaker population in Ireland peaked about the time of Mary's birth, numbers didn't translate into vitality. Spiritually the Society was at a low ebb, with most Quakers being only superficially involved (Harrison 12). But Neale grew up in a meeting that was "favored with a living and powerful ministry" (Samuel and Mary Neale 12). She had a "hard and impenitent heart" during her young years, followed by a sense of divine calling at age 17. In response to that call she engaged in travel and visitation, primarily among Friends, during the rest of her life.

Her desire as a traveling minister was to be grounded in God and to help others do the same in their individual lives, meetings and wider communities. Mourning the decline of the Religious Society of Friends, she functioned as "God's sharp threshing instrument," working for "the division in the society [of Friends] between the precious and the vile" (Mary Neale 68, 88).

Neale's early years of travel took her to Ireland and England. At age 36 she and a companion set out for America, arriving in South Carolina and traveling northward as far as Rhode Island. Her three years of traveling in America were extremely difficult for Neale because the customs and living conditions were so different from what she was used to. Travel by horseback and frequent illnesses took their toll. She was deeply troubled by the poor state of discipline, organization and spirituality in most meetings. Sometimes she was not well received.

A year after her return from America, Mary Peisley and Samuel Neale (1729-1792) declared their intentions of marriage. During the wedding both Samuel and Mary offered prayer and vocal ministry with great fervor. Two days later, to her husband's infinite grief, Mary Neale suddenly and unexpectedly died, being beset by a familiar stomach pain that had come back with vehemence. At her funeral, kneeling, her husband prayed powerfully; he includes many tributes to her in his journal.

In testimonies about Mary Neale written after her death, there is no mention of any official role or accomplishment attributed to her. Instead, there is appreciation for her faith. For example, in a tribute by her monthly meeting:

> She was a diligent laborer in spirit for the subjection of self and prevalence of Divine Life; and as she was very careful (when a

necessity was laid upon her) to rise up in that Life, so was she likewise to drop anchor, and sit down in it, more delighting in the pure silence of all flesh, and to hear the voice of her Beloved therein, than in any excellency of words.

The stories of Neale's travels in America include one brief reference to her belief that slavery is wrong (92), but there is no description of any anti-slavery efforts on her part. She visits backwoods people in North Carolina (88), but it's unclear whether any slaves were among them. Perhaps comments about slaves and slavery that were seen as controversial were edited out of her original journal. Such editing was common practice as journals of this era were passed down to succeeding generations (Bacon 13).

Mary's and Samuel's journals provide only a limited picture of their relationship. Among the many letters in these journals, there are none identified as being between Mary and Samuel. Mary was twelve years older than Samuel. While they may have been distant relatives (59), they were different in terms of social class, as he was a wealthy heir and landowner and she was from a modest background. Both were traveling ministers but neither of their journals refers to the support they may have offered each other for their traveling ministry. Samuel writes in his memoir that the idea of marriage occurred to him while he was listening to Mary speak at a meeting about her travels in America, shortly after her return (Samuel and Mary, 59, 66).

Mary's memoir does not mention John Woolman or his journal. Samuel's journal gives the impression that he was familiar with Woolman prior to meeting him on a trip to America after Mary's death, in 1771 (Samuel and Mary, 193-4). Historian Richard S. Harrison sees Samuel Neale as being less provincial than many Irish Friends, "in the same mold of Quaker character" as Woolman (13).

Broad Contextual Challenges Confronting Traveling Ministers

Large numbers of reforming ministers began traveling about 1750. One of their purposes was to awaken Friends to the need to reinforce the traditional discipline and business structures (Bacon 7). But the challenges they faced were much broader, including:

A. Denominationally, the need to retain the authenticity of the Quaker movement as it adapted to conditions of settled prosperity, which were in marked contrast to the early days of persecution and cataclysmic social change;

B. Theologically, the need to articulate and practice a Quietist stance reflecting Biblically-based assumptions about the nature of God's power;

C. Spiritually, the need for the traveling minister's connection with God to serve as a basis for encouraging others;

D. Communally, the need to develop a particularly Quaker methodology for visitation and ministry with communities of Friends.

Neale's approach to each of these challenges was grounded in her understanding of who God is and how God acts. Her writing cannot be appreciated apart from this frame of reference.

1. Retaining the authenticity of the Quaker movement as it adapted to new conditions

The faith and practice of eighteenth-century Friends was built on a foundation established by the first generation Friends (1646-66), whose experience was extremely intense. Through the manifestation of "the power of the Lord," early Friends felt "pierced in [their] inward parts," "melted into many tears," and "tendered together," brought about through God's "irresistible power" (Brinton 7-8). An early eyewitness account of Quaker worship describes "admiring auditors" standing and listening "like men astonished . . . as though every word was oracular; and so they believe them to be the very words and dictation of Christ" (Moore 144-5). The intensity of prayer was such that "we bore it long till the power of the Lord took hold upon us both and I was forced to cry out. . . There is a pure simplicity in them that would forgo all for the truth.. . .we are with them in fear and trembling lest their faith should stand in wisdom of words and not in the power of God" (Moore 147).

This first generation of Friends was able to confront their inner depths, overcome their particular weaknesses, and avoid the tendency to live deceitfully and selfishly (Ambler *Truth* 165). They could resist temptation and obey Christ's voice (Gwynn 69-70). Their experience of God's power went beyond the worship experience itself, resulting in healing of the infirm and change of heart by enemies (Ambler *Way* 108). They wrote letters overflowing with joy and tenderness even when confined in prisons that were "completely demoralizing and degrading" (Brinton 185).

As the years went by and the most severe persecution ended (1689), as Quakers became more settled and financially successful, as the vivid sense of social cataclysm and end-times eschatology faded away, the intensity of the Quaker movement quieted down. The focus shifted from surviving political persecution to practicing one's Quaker faith at home and protecting one's children from negative influences. By the eighteenth century, while reformers like Mary Neale were struggling to revive the legacy of the prior century, the larger Quaker community was working on developing "a consolidated sectarian spirituality" (Dandelion 53-7).

2. Articulating major theological beliefs

Through a word search I was able to generate a comparative list of texts based on the frequency of the phrase "the power of the Lord", considering all seventeenth- to nineteenth-century Quaker documents in the Digital Quaker Collection of the Earlham School of Religion. Neale's journal ranked higher than all other eighteenth-century documents. This is evidence of the extent of Neale's focus on God's power, in some ways hearkening back to the mindset of the first generation of Friends.

Neale's articulation of her experience of God's power is influenced by two major factors:

A. *The Bible*. Neale's approach reflects Biblical teachings about God's power, including the following: All power is derived from God, including secular political power and the powers of nature. It is God's nature and will to <u>act</u> in human history. God's power is greater than the power of evil. God grants autonomy to humans and to other entities. Humans can join with God in actively overcoming the misuse or perversion of the power that had originally been given by God for a better purpose. (*Interpreters Dictionary* 3.154).

B. *Quietism, a broad movement in Christianity that emphasizes interior passivity and receptivity to God*. From its earliest days, Quakerism has seemed compatible with Quietism due to its dichotomies between the things of God on one hand, and the things of "self" and "the world" on the other hand, which is evidenced in the writings of early Friends like Sarah Blackborow and Isaac Penington (Keiser and Moore 134, 203), and the *Apology* of Robert Barclay (1648-90).

The Quietistic period of Quaker history (beginning in the eighteenth century) was a time when putting self aside was particularly emphasized, and not always in a well-balanced way. The era's tendency towards narrowness and disengagement from the world is often criticized (Dandelion 59). Quietism is cautious about too much reliance on human reason (Dandelion 62; Cooper 59). Rufus Jones came to believe that an excessive rejection of reason in Quaker Quietism resulted in a system that was incapable of making decisions (Jones 155-161).

In contrast, Margaret Bacon points to some positive aspects of Quietism. It helped traveling ministers, including women such as Mary Neale, to experience themselves as liberated to address important issues. Eighteenth-century Quietism "did not mean inactivity; Quaker ministers traveled widely during this period, and the Quakers entered upon some of their most important reforms, such as work with the Native Americans and for the abolition of slavery during this time. But it meant an extreme emphasis on keeping self in abeyance" (14).

3. Maintaining the traveling minister's connection with God.

Mary Neale experienced God's power in many forms. When she speaks of the "power of truth" and the "power of love"—the "eternal," "baptizing," and "renewing" power—she understands these as manifestations of "the power of the Lord." Since connecting with God's power is more important than developing one's human abilities, Neale mentions supernatural power three times more often than she mentions human power or the powers of the world.

God's power as experienced by Neale was active. She describes how it "broke in upon us, to the comfort and refreshment of our souls," resulting in "a time of solemn worship" (Mary Neale 35). On one occasion, "even devilish spirits were made subject to that power by which we were assisted to speak" (88). Again and again, Neale emphasizes that God's power is essentially different from that which seems pleasing or comfortable to "the creature," that is, the person who is only operating out of his or her human nature.

> The general love and esteem that I met with for a time, which naturally drew my mind, and the prevalency of the love of God, which powerfully attracted my soul towards himself from all fading objects, that between these two powers, my mind was, at times, in that position that Absalom's body was, when he hung in a dying condition in the boughs of a tree, as between heaven and earth, scarce knowing which power would have me; but as there was a faithful obedience to the voice of the true shepherd, I found the power of Saul grow weaker, and that of David stronger. (Mary Neale 73)

As illustrated in the passages in the Appendix, Neale devotes tremendous energy to discerning and purging out of herself anything that might impede her receptivity to God and God's power.

4. Developing a Methodology for Working with Friends

Almost one-third of Neale's references to "power" take place in the context of a situation in which she is helping a person or group to go deeper. This is difficult work. She needs to continually remain in touch with God's power, but she finds the meetings to be far from God: places of "desolation, darkness and insensibility" (41). One meeting "groans under a dead lifeless ministry" (48). In another, Friends have "lost the spirit and power of godliness, but retain the form, being clothed with a pharisaical righteousness" (56). In another, "the disjointed members of our society . . . walk in the sight of their own eyes and the imagination of their own hearts, without being accountable to any for their conduct, and yet [are] called by the name of Quaker, to take away their reproach" (86).

In visiting meetings, Neal often experienced a painful loneliness, because she was so profoundly at odds with the people around her and with their expectations. This led her to a closer identification with Jesus.

When there was a need to say something challenging or difficult, Neale didn't back off. She sought divine guidance in enabling her to bring the uncomfortable truth out into the open, through what she calls "close work." As Drayton and Taber point out,

> "I had close work" meant that a minister was required by the Spirit to say difficult, embarrassing, or reprimanding things during a meeting or in a message during an opportunity in someone's home. . . . Close work may have originally meant "attentive" work, as in staying close to the Guide, despite the knowledge that what was being said was possibly difficult or upsetting to hear. . . . If the meeting was not well settled, and the minister was intensely aware that something was amiss, he or she might undergo "deep wading" in the labor to speak truthfully and fully as led to the condition of the meeting. (123, 220)

The following is a description of Neale's "close work":

> Close and hard work fell to our lots amongst those who called themselves of our society, which was difficult to be accomplished, because many thought themselves whole while . . . manifesting an

unlawful familiarity with the world . . . . We were led to endeavour to separate . . . some of the ruling members from the rest, to whom we had very close things to offer . . . . This seemed a very hard task to get accomplished because of their being so connected in marriage, &c. and the discipline being so sadly let fall, they knew not who were, or who were not proper members. (Mary Neale 106-7)

This type of "close work" seems not to have been practiced among Friends until the eighteenth century, in traveling ministers such as Thomas Elwood, Thomas Chalkley, John Woolman, John Churchman, Sarah Grubb, Mary Neale, Samuel Bownas, Job Scott, and Catherine Phillips. (Note: "close work" is also mentioned in the nineteenth-century journals of Martha Routh, Hannah Hall, Rachel Hicks and Ann Branson). Of the nine eighteenth-century journals listed above, only those of Mary Neale and Sarah Grubb include frequent references to both "the power of the Lord" and "close work."

Questions for further reflection

One can speculate on the factors that led to Mary Neale's particular way of focusing on "the power of the Lord." John Woolman's commitment to God was as intense as Neale's and he wrote a great deal about things related to God, but he didn't write so much about God's *power*. The word "power" is used 47 times in Neale's 120-page memoir, compared to 35 times in Woolman's 243-page journal. Neale and Woolman had a similar interest in the effects of God's power on their own life and ministry, but Woolman wrote much less often than Neale did about God's power operating in the Quaker community.

When she describes the effects of God's activity, Neale's writing style is simpler and more direct than Woolman's. She writes "God upheld me in my trials" (11) and "God caused my soul to taste of joys and consolation" (12). Woolman is more indirect and abstract when he uses language like "under a sense of God's Love I was comforted" (91). Woolman characteristically uses the phrase "a *sense* of something" to describe his own cognitive process of coming into deep awareness of some idea, inner state, or aspect of a larger truth. For example, he writes of "a *sense* of my own wretchedness" (138) and "an awful *sense* of God's goodness" (104).

There are 21 vignettes or anecdotes in Woolman's journal in which the "plot" of the vignette revolves around Woolman's experience of coming to terms with "a *sense* of something." The "something" may be positive or negative. The conflict to be resolved may be an inner, personal challenge (e.g. an inner state of weakness, turmoil, mourning, or unworthiness) or a practical problem in ministry. Comparing similar vignettes in Neale's memoir, both journals have twice as many vignettes revolving around the writer's inner state, compared to the number of vignettes describing concrete problems in the traveling ministry. This suggests that both writers are more focused on describing their inward state and their relationship with God than on providing guidance for dealing with concrete problems. Another similarity is that both writers end their vignettes by noting that the resolution of the conflict includes a gift from God of a deep inner peace.

In these vignettes, Woolman displays more interest in cognitive processes than Neale does. He writes about being affected by "a *sense* of something" 34 times, while Neale only mentions "a *sense* of something" seven times, and not in major passages.

This comparison between Neale and Woolman highlights Neale's single-minded and concrete way of focusing on God, which to her was the only thing that mattered. On the basis of her experience of God's power, Neale encouraged Friends to distance themselves from their own wishes and desires so that they could be more open to the ways of God, which she experiences as essentially different from human ways.

In my opinion, additional study of Mary Neale's memoir, and a fuller comparison of Neale's and Woolman's journals, could be fruitful. Some readers of Mary Neale may also want to explore what it would be like to follow her example of putting self aside in order to focus more fully on God's power in the lives of individuals and faith communities.

APPENDIX

Passages Describing Mary Neale's Experiences of Spiritual Empowerment

Accepting the necessity of her weakness and her suffering

[B]y the goodness and healing virtue of the Lord, I was often made to forget my bodily infirmities, and to see and feel that [God's] strength was made perfect in weakness. (89)

[I have] found the Lord my God deserts not the poor and mean of this world, but visits them in their lonely situations and humble retirements before him. This I am a witness of, for he was often with my spirit in this time of weakness; speaking peace and comfort to my soul, that could not live without him. One day in particular, as I rode to meeting, being much better in health, his living word, ran sweetly through my mind, thus, "For this purpose have I raised thee up, to shew forth in thee my power of preservation and mercy." [This] greatly rejoiced my soul, and caused me to praise his excellent name, (who is everlastingly worthy) for all his mercies. (61)

As I quietly rode along, the Lord was pleased in mercy to break in upon my mind by his living presence and power, and it became the language of my soul, "Speak, Lord, and thy servant will hear," after which many things were divinely opened to me, wherein I greatly rejoiced and was thankful to the Lord my God. I then found a sudden but gentle rebuke, and heard as it were a voice that said in the secret of my soul, "The dispensations thou most delightest in are least pleasing to me, and not so beneficial to thy soul as that pure poverty of spirit, brokenness and contrition of heart, which brings into humility of mind. And the reason why this is so little desired and so unpleasant to the creature is that it can have no part therein, but is wholly excluded and set at nought . . . and for this cause it is that I will in no wise despise the offering of a broken and contrite spirit." (44)

Waiting for God's action

. . . a concern rest[ed] with me to have another meeting in that city, which friends readily agreed to. The 15th had a meeting at Kirklington, which was large and satisfactory; and another at Carlisle in the evening, in consequence of the concern already mentioned, there came a great number of the town's folk; when I got there I found myself so weak in body and poor in spirit, and the people so unsettled in their minds, that I almost feared I should not be able to answer the service of the meeting. I earnestly desired that the cause and testimony of truth might not suffer, let me suffer what I might. I had not long sat, 'till I found a flow of doctrine open in my mind. I stood up in the fear of the Lord, and the people soon became quiet and solid. I was strengthened beyond my expectation, and the meeting ended well. And blessed be the name of the Lord, I had great peace and satisfaction after it was over. Went hence to [location], where my mind was under much suffering. But as I waited, the power of truth arose, and I found ease and liberty of mind; was led in a very close manner. (25)

Disengaging ("clearing herself") from a situation that interfered with her focus on God

. . . had a large meeting there; several friends coming from divers places to meet us, but that spirit was amongst them that obstructs the spring of the ministry and made it hard to speak. But by divine assistance, I was enabled to clear myself, and came away with peace of mind. (32-33)

The 28th had a large meeting. My Spirit was under deep suffering before I went to it, and for some time after, but, through divine aid, I fully cleared myself. When I came to my lodging, I was under a baptism of spirit, and could not tell the cause. I examined myself, and brought things to the closest scrutiny, to know whether I had done or omitted any thing contrary to truth, but could find no condemnation. At dinner, I felt the spirit of supplication, which I gave way to, and found my mind free and easy. (29-30)

✳ Works Cited ✳

Ambler, Rex, *The Quaker Way: A Rediscovery*, Winchester, UK: Christian Alternative Books, 2013. Print.

---. *Truth of the Heart*, London: Quaker Books, 2001. Print.

Bacon, Margaret Hope, Ed., *Wilt Thou Go on My Errand? Three 18th Century Journals of Quaker Women Ministers,* Wallingford, PA: Pendle Hill Publications, 1994. Print.

Brinton, Howard H. *Friends for 350 Years*. Wallingford, PA: Pendle Hill Publications, 2002. Print.

Cooper, Wilmer A., *A Living Faith: An Historical Study of Quaker Beliefs,* Richmond, IN: Friends United Press, 1990. Print.

Dandelion, Pink, *An Introduction to Quakerism*. Cambridge: Cambridge UP, 2007. Print.

Drayton, B. and W.P. Taber, Jr. *A language for the inward landscape: Spiritual wisdom from the Quaker movement*. Philadelphia: Tract Association of Friends, 2015. Print.

Gwynn, Doug, *Apocalypse of the Word: The Life and Message of George Fox,* Richmond, IN: Friends United Press, 1986. Print.

Harrison, Richard S. *A Biographical Dictionary of Irish Quakers*. Dublin: Four Courts Press, 1997. Print.

The Interpreter's Dictionary of the Bible, Nashville: Abingdon Press, 1962. Print.

Jones, Rufus M., *Quakerism, A Spiritual Movement*. Reprinted by Philadelphia Yearly Meeting, 1963. Print.

Keiser, R. Melvin and Rosemary Moore, *Knowing the Mystery of Life Within: Selected Writings of Isaac Penington in their Historical and Theological Context,* London: Quaker Books, 2005. Print.

Moore, Rosemary, *The Light in Their Consciences: the Early Quakers in Britain*, 1646-1666. State College: Penn State UP, 2000. Print.

Neale, Samuel and Mary: *Some Account of the Lives and Religious Labours of Samuel Neale and Mary Neale, Philadelphia,* a reprint of the first edition published in Dublin in 1805 and 1795.

Neale, Mary, *Some Account of the Lives and Religious Labours of Mary Neale,* ESR Digital Quaker Collection.

The Power of Story in Susanna Morris's Journal

by Marva L. Hoopes

It was a ministry staff retreat. The lead pastor asked us to list what things in ministry demanded our time in preparation, and then to evaluate the expenditure of that time. I jotted down, "Preparing and telling the children's story for Wednesday night" at the top of my list. Looking back over two decades in children's ministry, I realized much of my time involved telling stories. At our church's midweek program for children, I was the main storyteller for the large group. That retreat time of reflection and evaluation of ministry led to a study of the power of story. Was all that time spent in telling stories, time well spent? Had I been on the right track all those years? Did all those stories really make a difference in people's spiritual lives, or were they just entertaining? Was there truly power in a story? I suspected that there was, but I wondered if the practice of telling stories continued merely because "we've always done it this way" or if there was merit in continuing the use.

Story is a wildly popular theme in Christian education today. An abundance of Christian educational materials from numerous publishing companies have made their way onto the shelves of Christian bookstores and to online sources. People love stories; they read them, listen to them, watch them, and are entertained by them. But surely there is more to a story than mere amusement. Does a story have transformative power? What gives story its power, and how can that power best be used by Christian educators to further spiritual growth?

A story is understood as an account of the experiences of a certain character or characters in a chain of events moving through time and space, facing conflict and reaching resolution (Steffen; Fackre). In the church setting, stories told are often from the Bible, but churches also use mission stories, modern day dilemmas, heroes of the faith, and even classic stories from literature (May, et al.). In popular culture, a story is often viewed as fictitious, and in many instances this may be the case. Biblical stories, however, are held as true historical events that took place with genuine people, in actual places, as real, past experiences (Fee & Stuart).

As stories and their effects are analyzed, it is evident that stories have such great influence because of the way they impact various domains of human learning: cognitive, affective, behavioral, social, and spiritual. As stories are internalized and understood, they take root in these domains and as a result become transformative in their effect. Story has the power to affect the whole person—an influential medium indeed (Hoopes).

The Quaker Journal as Story

A person may tell his or her own story, and thus derive meaning and significance in the sharing. By the same token, a story may also be a historical account of a person's life experience, such as that of a person in history. In Quaker history, these often took the form of a journal in which the writer described experiences, lessons learned, and thoughts developed through the medium of the written word. Howard Brinton describes the development of Quaker journals as a religious autobiography in which the journalist's writings reflect an inner personal experience, charting stages of spiritual progress through life situations. Journal writers shared their thoughts and their stories and connected them with a biblical perspective, leaving them for future generations to ponder.

Susanna Morris (1682-1755)

One such journal writer is Susanna Morris, Quaker minister of the Gospel on both sides of the Atlantic in the seventeenth and eighteenth centuries. Born in England, Susanna was the oldest of five daughters of Susanna and Robert Heath. Moving to Pennsylvania in 1701, the family settled near Philadelphia and joined Abingdon Meeting. The family gave high priority to their Quaker faith as can be seen in the fact that four of the five daughters became ministers of the Gospel. In 1703 Susanna married Morris Morris in a Quaker ceremony at the Abingdon Meetinghouse in the presence of their families. Their first son was born a year later, and the couple eventually had twelve children, although four died when quite young.

Susanna's call to ministry began at age 29. With the blessing of her husband and the Quaker meeting, she traveled among Friends meetings in the colonies and even in Europe. She recorded a journal for her children and grandchildren, expressing deep faith and gratefulness, declaring it a testimony of God's goodness. She proclaimed her purpose in writing, stating:

> And now to my own travels, and good experiences of the Lord's help and many deliverances he has wrought for me herein are worthy of some note, yet I may not be able to set them forth as their worth is, but here and there a little as it is brought to my remembrance, I hope for the good of some weak ones. (Bacon 29)

Susanna writes humbly and attributes her successes and escapes from harm to God. She affirms God's divine goodness included protection from near fatal incidents, endowing wisdom to bring unity and reconciliation to various groups of Friends, granting the ability to give grace to enemies, and the ability to persevere in adverse circumstances. Her story is recorded in *Wilt Thou Go On My Errand? Three 18th Century Journals of Quaker Women Ministers: Susanna Morris (1682-1755), Elizabeth Hudson (1722-1783)*, and Ann Moore (1710-1783) by Margaret Hope Bacon. Susanna's journal is not only a riveting tale but is one from which many spiritual lessons can be learned.

Shipwrecked!

At forty years of age, Susanna answered God's call to visit Friends in Carolina, Virginia, and Maryland. Accompanied by Ann Roberts, they sailed across the Chesapeake Bay in 1722, but met with "hard and boisterous winds" and were driven out to sea. "… Had not the Lord favored us by an outstretched arm we had likely perished all of us that were in that vessel, for it was an open boat" (Bacon 42). They were driven across a sandbar, and the sea washed over them mercilessly. All their provisions had been soaked in salt water, resulting in the loss of food for the people and horses on board. Having lost his bearings, the captain did not know where they were. In time, they spotted land with a grassy area nearby. One man on a horse was dispatched to survey the area to see if there were any inhabitants nearby and if it was an island or the mainland. At the very least, it was thought, the horse could receive nourishment from eating the grass growing there. The man returned saying it was indeed an island and recommended they let the other horses graze on the grass as well. Strangely, when the horses were led out, they galloped off in the opposite direction quickly disappearing from sight.

Three days later, Susanna lay down on the deck in stillness and in prayer. She was suddenly prompted to get up and look around. She was surprised to note that two canoes were laboriously approaching. It took till the end of the day for them to reach the ship, and when they did, they promised to return the following day to help them. One man took them to shore, landing at the same place where they had taken the horses. He told them that there was a house six miles away where a poor widow lived but he could not take them there or stay with them. The weary travelers were becoming quite weak from not having eaten for the five days marooned on the shipwrecked vessel, but Susanna and Ann were undaunted and set out, determined to find the widow's house. When they finally could see the house, a half-mile away, they realized the path to the house had been destroyed; the sea had covered it up. At that moment, the widow appeared and met them saying, "Good women, how come ye hither? Was it to do the will of God?" She brought them into her home, where they spent the next several days under her nurturing care.

Susanna and Ann discovered that their horses were a mere quarter of a mile from the widow's house! The horses could have been 100 miles away by this time, but there they were, right near them, in spite of the numerous mosquitoes that infested the area. The women rode the horses bareback in return to the ship to collect their saddles and clothing. Susanna blithely recounts that this "at other times might have been a great hardship but surely the Lord makes hard things easy for those that are willing to serve him well" (Bacon 45). God had delivered them from a dangerous and life-threatening crisis. God is faithful and trustworthy.

Ministry to bring unity and reconciliation

In 1729, Susanna and Ann traveled to Europe, ministering to Friends in Ireland, England, and Holland. In Holland they could not speak the language and had to work through interpreters, which they found quite tedious.

In the Twisk area of North Holland, the ministers were distressed to find a great problem of disunity among Friends. Although there was but one meeting, it was divided between two different leaders. For over ten years each minister had gathered half of the meeting at their respective houses. The interpreter had tried to hide this fact from the visiting women but a member of the group met with the women to discuss the sensitive issue. Susanna recorded that a "solid man full of grief (as we were)… told us his trouble" (Bacon 53). He felt the women could be instrumental in reuniting the people. Susanna and Elizabeth traveled to Amsterdam to meet with one of the ministers involved. After much convincing, they were able to accompany him to Twisk in order to seek reconciliation. Several successful meetings resulted in the Friends sensing forgiveness, peace, and love with each other, glad that the women had been sent to them.

Susanna's clear point from this encounter is this:

> I write this account for the future so all of us may beware of letting in anything of that kind that would separate but rather as pillars of God's house suffer and with patience bear until his holy hand may turn things that seemed to go across to our minds into order again. (Bacon 53-54)

Peace and unity are crucial in God's perspective. God had used Susanna and Ann as agents of reconciliation.

Praying for their enemies and experiencing God's protection

When Susanna was 62 years old, she felt another calling by God to return to the European continent on his errand. The grueling journey took just over two months to cross the Atlantic. Sailing from Ireland to England in April 1745, their route took them past the Isle of Man. In the distance, another vessel appeared, looking very much like it could be an enemy ship. As it neared, the ship sailed one time around them, and then another way around them, looking quite threatening. At first Susanna was quite shocked at this, but then she was prompted to pray and believe that God would discourage the potential enemies. She was then overwhelmed by a concern for these people she did not even know, and prayed that God would give them grace and would "influence them with his Holy Spirit to do justice and love mercy for his name's sake" (Bacon 65). She realized that it pleases God when we pray for our enemies. The other ship never did attack them. After arriving safely in England, they heard reports about nasty pirate attacks that had occurred in the very area where they had sailed and realized they had indeed been spared.

In 1746, Susanna was returning to Pennsylvania from London. It would have been safer to avoid sailing past Scotland, since enemy French ships had taken over 25 ships in the area. However, the winds were more favorable to sail in that direction and the captain decided to take that route "without council of any man." Susanna, however, claimed that she trusted in "a far better arm than all the contrivance of men and all that the arm of flesh can do for them" (Bacon 81). Twice they encountered French ships and the crew readied guns on the ship. But the ships turned away and they were saved from danger. Susanna gave all the praise to the goodness of God who cares for his servants.

Crossing the Atlantic, crosswinds kept them from quickly landing on American shores. After their delay in arriving, they learned that many French ships had been in those waters. Susanna claimed that the Lord had a good end in it after all, in providing those cross winds to keep them safe from any harm.

We can trust God in precarious situations. Praying for those seen as enemies is what pleases God.

Saved from danger at sea – again and again!

During one of her many voyages to the European continent, a great storm arose and their ship was run aground on the coast of Holland. All night the vessel took many hard strokes on the sands, battered by the wind and the waves. The distressed passengers spent all night in the cold, stormy water, hanging on for dear life to the ship's parts. In the darkness, Susanna's companion, Sarah Lay, gripped Susanna, saying they were so in fellowship with one another that if she must die, she would rather go with Susanna. In the morning they were able to raise a flag of distress and the people of nearby city of Enkhuizen came to rescue them. Susanna concludes the story with praise to God, who had helped them through this great hardship, saying,

> The Lord much sweetened my many bitter cups not only formerly, but also in this journey and I have thought that none of the Lord's servants could well say that they had suffered enough, for the God of the living best knows when our sufferings are all gone through, but the best ye my children can do or for anyone else that truly are bent to follow the Lord through many trials is this: Let them shut their hearts up against the flesh, and steadily turn to the God of true hope, for he is able to help through all hardships. Therefore, oh let all trust in him the Lord Jehovah, for in him is everlasting strength, blessed be his name forever and ever and to his praise may I yet say. (Bacon 72)

On yet another voyage, Susanna traveled in December with several British Friends ministers, who were returning to England. During times of meditation and prayer, Susanna had several spiritual impressions of being shipwrecked. At first she did not want to believe it, and wondered if others had the vision as well. She realized she was alone in receiving the impression and when the "dream" came again and yet again, she was convinced it was from the Lord. She compared her situation to the women bearing the news of Christ's resurrection to the doubting disciples. Shaking with fear from the memory of previous shipwrecks at sea, Susanna experienced God's peaceful reassurance that the waves would not hurt them and God would preserve them. Hesitantly she shared her vision with the startled captain, but assured him that she also saw him safe on shore in the end. When the weather turned foul and storm conditions overwhelmed the ship, the captain valiantly tried to maintain its course but it was run into rocks off the coast of Ireland and thrown on its side. Some were drowned in the disaster and the remaining survivors all hung desperately onto parts of the ship, trying to find the highest place to avoid being swept away by the waves and water. Suddenly, Susanna sensed they should all move to the lower side of the ship. Although it took much convincing, when the survivors moved to what seemed like the more precarious side, huge waves crashed on the high side of the ship and destroyed it. No one was lost because they had moved to safety. Nine long hours were spent in the dark and angry sea. When morning came the townspeople appeared and rescued the surviving crew and passengers. Since this was a Catholic area, some felt fearful of harm, but the local priest had declared that they should treat the survivors as respectfully and honorably as they might treat the Holy Father himself. The gracious rescuers sent letters to Friends in the surrounding area who came with provisions and offers of shelter. When Susanna's role became known, she was hailed as a hero and spiritual authority. Many came to hear her speak as she made her way through the towns and provinces in Ireland and England.

Strength and wisdom through difficult times

At 70 years of age, Susanna felt drawn to make one more trip to England to minister in some of the places she had not yet visited in the southwestern area. She visited nearly 50 different meetings from May 1752 to September 1753. Travel was not easy. She writes:

> I visited all down the south parts of the west of England from Portsmouth to Land's End, though a very hilly country and bad roads, I thought it was very hard for me to get up and down the hills, for some of them were more like to stairs in an house than any other thing, and so stony that my creature threw me off many times, but (forever blessed be my great Master and preserver) I was never much hurt and sometimes not hurt at all; for the creature bowed herself so low with me that it was like laying me down and the last time it was in the soft mud. (Bacon 98)

On this trip Susanna constantly spoke Truth to Friends as well as to those not yet convinced. She shared the Gospel with all who would listen, and many did listen to this courageous woman who spoke with authority and wisdom. She was not afraid to speak out against worldly temptations, such as use of tobacco and liquor, and urged people to be filled with the Spirit instead. She encountered disbelief that the Lord would use females to labor in the Gospel and affirmed that God is willing and able to use women to go on his errands.

At times she battled homesickness, being away from her family for as many as three years at a time. But she didn't allow herself to wallow in pity, desiring instead to remain a faithful witness to God's strength and help.

> And then my mind began to go a little too fast home, for I was ready to say in my heart, O let me go home again if I must come back again but I can well think it was not good for me to think so, therefore let none that would do the best they can take example by me in that. (Bacon 61)

In her shipwreck experiences Susanna was able to rely on God to be a source of comfort and strength. Honor is constantly given to God in each difficult situation. As Susanna relates her story, the reader is continually encouraged to place trust in the Almighty God.

> Therefore let my soul bless and praise the living God who has been pleased to do for me a poor unworthy creature than ever I could either have asked of him or thought of. Although I have had many, yea, more than common deliverances both by shipwreck at sea and various trials at land in my pilgrimage thus far through time, yet I find it still safe for me and I believe all the children of my Father's house to think little of themselves, for all the good that any of us are capable of doing from the ability that the God and Father of all our mercies bestoweth on us for his own honour's sake only. (Bacon 64)

The Power of Story – As Seen through this Quaker Journal

Susanna's story is a legacy of an amazing woman who trusted God and was mightily used for his sake. She reports that through the Lord's goodness she was able to experience "victory over all wrong spirits and hope [that she] had some good service amongst them" (Bacon 99). Susanna's story is powerful. She writes with an intentionality that has a significant influence in shaping values, spiritual development, and faith. As her children, grandchildren, and all who come after her read her journal, they are struck with the power of her experiences and her words. As readers are immersed in her story, it prompts faith and service to God. Her narrative touches the whole person. In the cognitive realm, ways of thinking about God are expanded and deepened. In the affective realm, the personal relationship with God is enriched and enhanced. In the behavioral realm, ways of responding to crises and difficult situations are modeled. In the social realm, ways of relating to fellow women and men are practiced and displayed for the reader to emulate. And in the spiritual realm, the thanks, praise, glory, and honor are always directed to God. The reader is swayed to follow Susanna's example of humility and devotion to the Savior through her powerful testimony. Susanna's shared experiences allow the reader to live them through her words and descriptions. Insight into God's character, actions, and design for life is gained. In reading Susanna's journal, we see how she finds her place in God's grand story, and we find ours as well.

Read the journals of other courageous and outstanding Quaker women in:

Wilt Thou Go On My Errand? Three 18th Century Journals of Quaker Women Ministers: Susanna Morris, Elizabeth Hudson, Ann Moore, edited by Margaret Hope Bacon. Pendle Hill Publications, 1994.

Hidden in Plain Sight – Quaker Women's Writings (1650-1700), edited by Mary Garman, Judith Applegate, Margaret Benefiel, Dortha Meredith. Pendle Hill Publications, 1996.

Strength in Weakness – Writings by Eighteenth Century Quaker Women, edited by Gil Skidmore. AltaMira Press, 2003.

✳ Works Cited ✳

Bacon, Margaret Hope. *Wilt thou go on my errand? Three 18th century journals of Quaker women ministers*. Wallingford, PA: Pendle Hill Publications, 1994. Print.

Brinton, Howard H. *Quaker journals: Varieties of religious experiences among Friends*. Wallingford, PA: Pendle Hill Publications, 1972. Print.

Fackre, Gabriel. *The Christian story: A narrative interpretation of basic Christian doctrine* (Rev. ed.). Grand Rapids, MI: William B. Eerdmans, 1984. Print.

Fee, Gordon. D. & Douglas Stuart. *How to read the Bible for all its worth: A guide to understanding the Bible* (2nd ed.). Grand Rapids, MI: Zondervan, 1993. Print.

Hoopes, Marva. L. "The power of story in the spiritual development of children." Diss. Talbot School of Theology, Biola University, 2013. Print.

May, Scottie, Beth Posterski, Catherine Stonehouse, & Linda Cannell. *Children matter: Celebrating their place in the church, family, and community*. Grand Rapids, MI: William B. Eerdmans, 2005. Print.

Steffen, Tom A. *Cross-cultural storytelling at home and abroad: Reconnecting God's story to ministry*. Waynesboro, GA: Authentic Media, 2005. Print.

✳3| Quakers, Modernism, and Action✳

Recovering Pacifisms Past: Modernist Networks, the Society of Friends, and the Peace Movement of the Spanish Civil War

by J. Ashley Foster

> ...*the future is always seen from somewhere ... past hopes and preparations for the future, although they recede, may be recovered and rehabilitated as resources in the present. History, that is, may be a repository of forgone possibilities, unrealized desiderata, utopias that keep feeding our plans.*

> Paul Saint-Amour, *Tense Future*

> *I shall never forget this host of men and women, fighting a new kind of battle behind the men at the front, fighting for a disciplined, educated new generation that will be equipped to build Spain anew, above the wrecks and waste of war.*

> S. Emily Parker, *From the Devotional Diary of A Relief Worker in Spain*

Battles waged on many fronts in Spain during the Civil War of 1936-1939. The fascist bombings of Madrid, Almeria, Valencia, and Guernica became emblematic of the way in which total war (where civilians become military targets) invaded the cities, homes and lives of the people, collapsing distinctions between traditional "war" and "safety" zones. Battles waged on many fronts in Spain, but Emily Parker, a relief worker with the American Friends Service Committee (AFSC), captures in her diary a new kind of battle. When war in Spain broke out, though thousands of internationally concerned citizens volunteered to fight for the Spanish Republic in the International Brigades, an alternative conglomerate of workers, individuals, artists, activists, and societies organized in reaction to the military forces on the ground. Artists, writers, and volunteers came together for peace and human rights, for social justice and global equality, "fighting a new kind of battle behind the men at the front" (*Devotional Diary* 7). This spontaneous, diffuse, non-hierarchal army for peace[1] materialized a pacifism that was most certainly not passive and provides an archive of pacifisms past[2] that can help us build a vocabulary of peace towards the future. It unveils an intricate network of modernist thinkers, authors, and artists working alongside the Society of Friends, relief organizations, and fundraising communities in an attempt to spread peace throughout first Spain, and then the world.

The war in Spain, due to repeated bombings of the civilian population, posed an ethical and moral "challenge to pacifism."[3] A group of generals on a far-right platform, eventually to be lead by the dictator Francisco Franco, with support of the military, church, and landowners, rebelled against the democratically-elected, fledgling Republican Government on July 17-18, 1936. The coup d'état failed when the people formed workers' militias and fended off the professionally trained military. Reinforcements arrived from Russia and the International Brigades. Support from Germany and Italy came to the rebels' aid and Russia got involved on the side of the Republic; Spain quickly became an international affair. Seen by the intellectual left as a battle against fascism, and by the right as a fight against secularization and Godlessness, global passions concerning Spain ran high. When the fascists starting bombing civilian populations, many of the world community responded with moral outrage.[4] In

---

[1] Kathleen Innes, a prominent Quaker peace activist of the time, in *The Prevention of War*, discusses how pacifist thought called for a "Peace Army" during the Sino-Japanese conflict (69).

[2] This phrase "pacifisms past" is also an echo of Saint-Amour's analysis of Woolf's "Thoughts on Peace in an Air Raid," where Saint-Amour argues that Woolf's essays calls us to "be blown backward into the future with your gaze fixed on past wars and past writing, as well as on *peacetimes past*" (emphasis mine 130).

[3] This is the name of a pamphlet published in 1937 written by H. Runham Brown, the Secretary of the War Resisters' International. While it acknowledges the challenge Spain presents, it upholds a commitment to peace.

[4] For a more complete history of the Spanish Civil War, see Paul Preston's *The Spanish Civil War: Reaction, Revolution, and Revenge*; Helen Graham's *The War and its Shadow: Spain Civil War*

protest of Britain's, France's and the United States' non-intervention policy, the global intellectual left were predominantly supporting movements like "Arms for Spain" and the volunteers of the International Brigades who enlisted to fight on the front lines against fascism in Spain.[5] The story that modernist studies, in its historical reconstruction of the era, tells of the interwar era is of an early 1930's thriving pacifist movement that gives way to mass militarization mobilization as Adolf Hitler and Benito Mussolini start to support the rebellion in Spain and fascism grows. As Sarah Cole so elegantly puts it, "The pacifist watches, admist a dwindling circle of friends, as war engulfs not only the continent but his own political movement" (227).[6]

While this metanarrative does have truth to it, there were also a number of modernist artists, intellectuals, and activists who, instead of supporting war in Spain, joined together in causes for peace and social justice, linked by their shared commitment to raise funds for and provide relief to refugees, particularly children. Based on the belief that peace, like war, is a *choice*, they aspired to change the consciousness of the people.[7] Art and literature, at the time, were seen as ways of intervening in cultural discussions, as ways of shaping public conversations, and therefore had the potential to influence policy.[8] The Quakers, also known as the Society of Friends, a religious group

---

in Europe's Long Twentieth Century and *The Spanish Civil War: A Very Short Introduction*. For more on bombings in Spain, see Ian Patterson's *Guernica and Total War*.

[5] Nancy Cunard's pamphlet *Authors Take Sides on the Spanish Civil War* illustrates the way in which the British intellectual community primarily and vocally supported the Republic. The survey asked British authors: "Are you for, or against, the legal Government and the People of Republican Spain? Are you for, or against, Franco and Fascism?" Out of 148 responses, 16 proclaimed they were "neutral," only 5 declared support for Franco, and an overwhelming 127 averred support for the Republic, many of them quite passionately.

[6] Stanly Wientraub declared that the war made pacifism "intolerable" (9). Angela Jackson's *British Women and the Spanish Civil War* tells how "those who had been particularly responsive to the idea of pacifism were faced with a crisis of conscience. As their belief in the possibility of peace through collective security in the League of Nations began to fade, many modified their views to allow for the necessity of fighting in a 'just war' in response to the rise of the fascist dictators" (42). These are just a few examples of how the historical narrative tells of a disintegrating peace movement with the rise of fascism.

[7] One compelling example of this belief is the document "War and Writers," pasted in Virginia Woolf's reading notebooks. It states: "The time has come for all those who care for the well-being of our civilization to take resolute action for peace. In this work, a special opportunity, a special duty, falls to the writers in all countries. They can try to undermine the war mentality and spread the spirit of peace" (Monks House Papers/B.16f. Vol. 2 [Sussex] 28).

[8] Paul Robeson's famous speech, "The Artist Must Take Sides," delivered at the *Spain & Culture Rally* on June 24, 1937, exemplifies this argument for the role the artist has in shaping consciousness and politics. He proclaims: "the true artist cannot hold himself aloof. The legacy of culture from our predecessors is in danger… May your inspiring message reach every man, woman, and child who stands for freedom and justice" (119).

with Protestant roots known for their pacifism, produced numbers of pamphlets advocating for peace and support of relief work in Spain during the 1930's. Virginia Woolf not only published her modernist peace pamphlet *Three Guineas* during the height of the trauma in Spain (1938), she supported the National Joint Committee for Spanish Relief, which raised funds to give food and milk to refugees that the Quaker relief workers on the ground distributed. Duncan Grant and Angelica (Woolf's niece), Quentin (Woolf's nephew) and Vanessa Bell (Woolf's sister) all worked closely with the Artists International Association, which also supported the National Joint Committee and many Aid Spain campaigns.

This paper puts modernist pacifisms, particularly the socialist, feminist pacifism of Virginia Woolf and the Quaker pacifism of the early twentieth century, in conversation with the Aid Spain relief network, particularly the distribution of food conducted by the Society of Friends. Quaker philosophy, methodology, networks, and organization, I argue, were an essential component to a nascent, and at times secular, transitional European pacifism whose roots can be traced to the outbreak of the First World War and grew in the interwar years. This pacifist thought of the early twentieth century was manifested in the works of the great literary minds such as Virginia Woolf and her Bloomsbury community. Woolf engaged in the cultural conversations of her time to construct a peace based on social and economic equality and to fight the oppressions and tyranny of a rising fascism. She did so by writing and thinking. She invents the "Outsiders' Society" (*Three* 126) in her polemical peace pamphlet *Three Guineas*, an "antisociety" (Introduction *lviii*) composed of the "daughters of educated men" (*Three* 16) who work for peace in the world. It is my contention, and what I will develop for the rest of this article, that Woolf's fictional "Society of Outsiders" (130), a group of women dedicated to the promotion of peace, committed to fighting for "the rights of all" (Woolf quoting Josephine Butler, 121), has its real life manifestation and corollary in the positive peace effort that sprung up around the Spanish Civil War in the Aid Spain movement.

The lost pacifisms past, or as Paul Saint-Amour quotes Reinhart Koselleck, of "futures past" (31) that I recuperate in this paper challenge and exceed the notion of pacifism as an absence of war. Pulling upon the both/and structure, and exploring the tensions and traces of *différance* within pacifism(s), pacifism is both an absence of war, but more so, and more importantly, an active creation that can set the conditions for a lasting peace. Upon the outbreak of the Spanish Civil War, women came together all over the world and created a transnational network of pacifist activism that sought to build conditions where peace could flourish in a variety of ways, each bearing witness to their own, individually held, Peace Testimony. "Testimony" is a Quaker term that signifies lived practices that enact inner beliefs. The Quaker Peace Testimony stems from the Quaker belief of the Inner Light[9]—that there is that of good, or that of God, in every person,[10] and therefore extinguishing that Light by taking another's life is profoundly wrong. The Peace Testimony would therefore be the actions taken to manifest the inner beliefs of pacifism within-the-world, a set of practices, acts, and deeds that combat violence and support the thriving and flourishing of the Inner Light.[11] When I say that women artists and women in the Society of Friends who operated the relief efforts in Spain, manifested their personal expressions of an individually held Peace Testimony, I am arguing that these women came together to forge a pacifism based on lived, constructive actions. This activist pacifism, or as the discipline of peace studies would say "positive peace," is the construction of a world that can sustain peace, social systems based on freedom, and racial, gendered, and financial equality. In a similar logic, Farah Mendlesohn's comprehensive study, *Quaker Relief Work in the Spanish Civil War*, develops the idea that in the nineteenth and early twentieth century the Peace Testimony of the Society of Friends progressively adopted a social justice component, shifting from an emphasis on the absence of war to a goal of creating the conditions for a lasting peace.[12] As

---

[9] Pink Dandelion discusses the history of the term "Inner Light," explaining that it is "mainly a twentieth-century invention" (133). An appropriation of the "inward Light of earlier generations" (132), Inner Light "became normative through the influential writings of Rufus Jones who used it interchangeably with 'inward Light'" (133). Because this paper focuses on the modernist Friends and early twentieth century Quaker thought and action, I feel it is the term most suited to describe the foundational beliefs of Quaker thought during the interwar era.

[10] Caroline Emelia Stephen, Virginia Woolf's Quaker theologian aunt, describes the Inner Light as, "there is given to every human being a measure, or germ, of something of an illuminating nature—something of which the early Friends often spoke as 'a seed of life'—a measure of that 'light, life spirit and grace of Christ' which they recognized as the gift of God to all men" (*Light* 2).

[11] *The Historical Dictionary of the Friends (Quakers)* defines "testimony" as "the public witness of actions, beliefs, and behaviors that Friends hold to be consistent with **Truth**" (340). The dictionary explains, "Friends came to understand in the early years of the movement that the spirit of Christ would never move a person to kill either for human kingdoms or for the kingdom of God... they lived under the new **covenant** whereby all people would come to live in peace. This belief was at the root of what has come to be known as the Friends **peace testimony**" (258-259).

[12] Mendlesohn explains: "The AFSC [American Friends Service Committee] and the FSC [Friends Service Council] were products of the acceptance of a social gospel which put deeds before words... Liberal Quaker theology emphasized social justice as a crucial element in the making of peace... in their work in Europe and Ireland during the nineteenth century, the Friends had moved from a belief in the keeping of peace through neutrality and non-

Mendlesohn shows, the emphasis on social justice became an important part of the peace mission of the Quakers; similarly, the pacifism of modernist artistic networks emphasized it as well.[13]

Reading the women of the Aid Spain movement as one real life manifestation of the Society of Outsiders illuminates the integration of social justice activity into the modernist pacifist effort and opens the way for us to see how the operation of the Society of Outsiders in the Spanish Civil War work accedes to an "intimate ethics" and notions of global responsibility for and to the other. It also highlights the way in which members of the Society of Friends were engaged with humanitarian issues of their contemporary moment and are actively intertwined within transnational networks that strove to envision and create the world that ought to be. First, this paper will outline notions of ontological responsibility as discussed by Judith Butler and the philosophy of "intimate ethics," as described by Jessica Berman, and establish why a feminist analysis of women thinkers and relief workers during the Spanish Civil War is particularly important and beneficial to this frame. It will proceed to trace some background of the interrelationship between the Society of Friends and modernist artistic networks during the interwar years, illustrating that the Quakers and modernist thinkers were a part of the same political groups, publishing houses, and activist societies. Then, I will show how "intimate ethics" is enacted on the ground in Spain through the accounts from women relief workers, and how this transnational network of activists operates as a real-life manifestation of Virginia Woolf's "Society of Outsiders." Finally, this study will close with how these Spanish Civil War pacifisms are relevant to the present day.

---

compliance in the acts of war, to a growing belief that it was their duty to make the conditions for peace" (159).

[13] Both Grace Brockington and Jean Mills make a substantial contribution to modernist studies by approaching modernist art and writing though this analytic of positive peace. Arguing for a theory of "pacifist modernism" (3), Grace Brockington shows how "advocates of positive peace argued that the peace movement must be constructive, not simply reactive, promoting social, political and cultural reform to eradicate the causes of war" (2) through the works of modernist artists Vanessa Bell, Duncan Grant, Roger Fry, and a number of others. Jean Mills's work on Virginia Woolf and Jane Ellen Harrison shows that their works "attend" to "this conception of peace as positive, with an emphasis on analyses of the conditions necessary for peace, such as conflict transformation and conflict resolution via such mechanisms as peace-building, peace-making, mediation, and conflict resolution" (136).

The Ethical Call For A Feminist Pacifist Analysis

Where is there a better place to observe Goodwill Day than in war-torn Spain? It brings one's idealism up against cold hard facts... What do we have to say today? For those of us who believe in a way of life not based on violence this is a very real and searching question. We are called to an accounting...

S. Emily Parker,
From the Devotional Diary of a Relief Worker in Spain

Violence against the other is a form of violence against our very self. This violence calls us, as Emily Parker has written, "to an accounting" (9), casting our ontological debts into full relief, thrusting the full weight of global citizenship upon our shoulders. Another way to say this would be that in the reflection of the bomb fire of Spain, the violence against civilians, the fratricide that occurred on the front lines, the attempted "obliteration"[14] of entire populations, and the international situation that allowed Hitler and Mussolini to evolve their battle tactics,[15] a cry of anguish echoed throughout the world, a cry that carried with it the imperative to end the suffering. It was a cry that carried with it the imperative of non-violence, which, according to Judith Butler, "arrives as an address or an appeal" (165). From whom does this appeal emerge, however, and as Butler asks, "under what condition are we responsive to such a claim" (165)?

As Butler develops in her post 9-11 book *Frames of War: When is Life Grievable,* the "appeal" of non-violence follows the register of an ethical call, which originates from our very existence as humans, in other words, from Being itself and the precariousness of our lives on this planet. Butler's point of departure is two-fold: 1) our human bodies are vulnerable, precarious entities and 2) this vulnerability both casts us into a social matrix of "unwilled proximity and interdependency" (*xxx*) and into an ethical struggle to subvert, redirect, or rechannel our violent potential and answer the possibility, or potentiality, for violence with non-violence. For Butler, we must start thinking of our bodies and ourselves-as-subjects as beings enmeshed in each other, ontologically reliant upon the social systems that sustain us and our world—this ontological interrelatedness is the source of our responsibility. We have a responsibility to create a world that can support and sustain the lives around us,

---

[14] This is Ian Patterson's thesis in *Guernica and Total War*–that total war was carried out with the intention of obliterating the enemy.

[15] Ernest Hemingway famously called the Spanish Civil War "the dress rehearsal for the inevitable European war" (qtd. in Martin,11).

for "the subject that I am is bound to is the subject I am not, that we each have the power to destroy and to be destroyed, and that we are bound to one another in this power and this precariousness. In this sense, we are all precarious lives" (43).

Throughout *Frames of War*, Butler demonstrates that who we see as interconnected and interrelated is preconditioned and informed through social channels and norms; in other words, who we see as human beings is predicated on whose lives are "grievable" and whose are not. This is the way in which war continues—we are formed by social iteration to distinguish between "those populations on whom my life and existence depend, and those populations who represent a direct threat to my life and existence. When a population appears as a direct threat to my life, they do not appear as 'lives,' but as the threat to life" (42). However, as previously stated, the ethics of non-violence is the call to resist violent potential, to find another way of responding. This ethics can only manifest, however, "from the apprehension of equality in the midst of precariousness" (181)–can only be realized in the refusal of frames that dehumanize entire populations and cast them out to be the enemy. This leaves us with the task of "a rethinking of responsibility" (33) that asks "how do we understand what it means to be a subject who is constituted in or as its relations, whose survivability is a function and effect of its modes of its relationality" (49)? If "war is precisely an effort to minimize precariousness for some and to maximize it for others" (54), then it follows that one of the ultimate refusals of the war-making system is to deny all claims that the other's lives are not, in fact, lives at all. The ultimate refusal of war, indeed, would then be to insist upon the other's humanity, and to answer the call of an ethical responsibility to sustain the social infrastructure that supports their lives— food, clothes, heat, soap, education, and work. When the Spanish Civil War broke out, the Quakers went to Spain in an ultimate gesture of defiance; instead of sending arms, they brought food; instead of choosing sides, they worked in both Republican and fascist territory; instead of turning Spain into a tragedy of masses of people, they sent letters back to London and Philadelphia filled with stories of individuals who were helped one-by-one. The Quaker Testimony for Peace, based on the belief in the Inner Light—that there is that of good or that of God in every individual—manifested in Spain as a fierce activist pacifism that tried to honor the sanctity of every human life in its worship of a divine spirit. The Quakers believed that, "A helping hand extended now without regard to political side or faction will save innocent lives—and more. It will pave the way to restored sanity in Spain and peace on earth" (*Give for Spain*). In this way, the Quaker pacifism of the Spanish Civil War manifested an "intimate ethics" that was also integral to the feminist pacifism of the modernist era.

Jessica Berman, in *Modernist Commitments*, develops this idea of "intimate ethics" in her chapter on Virginia Woolf and Jean Rhys. Citing Luce Irigaray and Tina Chanter's arguments addressing the "ethical intimacy of care" (44), Berman extends upon their argument that an ethical focus on care and concern "brings women to the center of ethics, where the Western philosophical tradition has rarely placed them" (44). Intimate ethics departs from the premise that "the self comes into being intersubjectively" (43) and that, and here Berman quotes Nancy, the "'essence of Being is only as co-essence" (45). In other words, pulling upon the Heideggerian metaphysical tradition, Being-with is a constitutive, primordial state—the self is constituted by and manifested within a community of others. This self and the other are cultivated through their embodied and grounded Being-in-the-world. In Berman's language, "the ethical, relational self begins from the reciprocity of our material appearance among others in the world and our embodied experiences of community" (46).

There is a responsibility, an ontological demand that accompanies "being toward the other in a bodily sense" (44), which starts at the "moment of the caress" (44) that is the "moment of recognition" (44) of the interconnectedness of our material, bodily co-essence. Consistent with Butler's logic, ontologically, our bodies and our selves are caught in a web of interdependence, recognized in the touch towards or of the other, which is the basis of ethical relations. When the other, then, suffers extreme violence to their bodies, when the material conditions that support their social structures are under attack, there is an ontological call from Being itself to respond. To extend Berman's logic, the way in which one responds directly to this call though embodied channels— touch, care, caress, or the handing one a cup of cocoa—is one realization of intimate ethics. The other, informed by Butler's *Giving an Account of Oneself*, no less important, "may also be understood as the scene of narration, which makes its reciprocal, ethical claims on teller and listener" (46). Both "scenes" are comprised by direct relations, proximity, and the emphasis on the resonances and influences of personalized and reciprocal care and touch—values, arguably, that women have historically materialized. There is an apprehension of an interplay between the self and other, and how the self is constituted by the very other. War, in particular total war, puts all these channels under erasure, eroding the community, and breaking down the material networks of survival, and it stages an assault on the ethics of care and intimacy that is called into being when two bodily entities face each other. Berman illustrates Virginia Woolf's resistance to the war-making system through her Society of Outsiders and an intimate ethics, concluding that, "Like the Society of Outsiders that Woolf imagines at the end of *Three Guineas*... the essay's involuted and interrupted narrative logic not only brings intimate ethics to bear on the public politics of antiwar activism but also acts as a political refusal of the very categories of identity created by and perpetuated in war and patriarchy" (76). For Berman, *Three Guineas'* use of narrative "gaps" (63), the fact that Woolf refuses to empathize with those who call for war, asserts an intimate ethics into the political discourse in the text and seeks to imagine a "better future of social relations" (84).

Woolf's fictional Outsiders' Society, and the real-life actualization of it, then, that organizes in response to total war in Spain denies and refuses the war-making system by enacting an intimate ethics, an ethics that recognizes the responsibility that we have to preserve and care for the body of the other. For Woolf, women will be the ones to lead the cause against war because they do not have an investment in the structures of power that benefit from perpetuating war. Tracing the roots of war to the patriarchy, capitalism, and imperialism, Woolf argues that because women have historically been kept "outsiders" (35) to this system, they have a perspective and opinion, an ability to "criticize" (21) that constitutes the "new weapon" (21) against war.

(See Figure 1, next page)

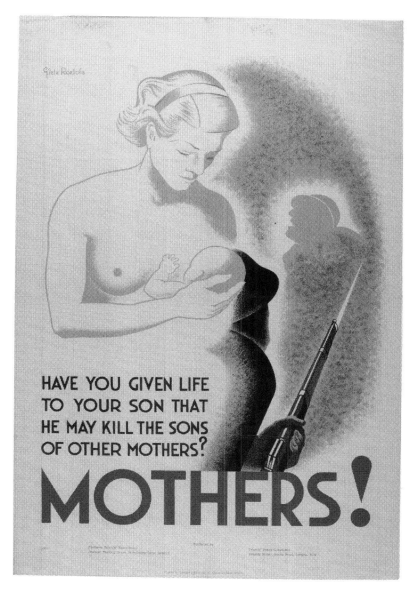

(Figure 1. "Mothers! Have you given life to your son that he may kill the sons of other mothers?" (Poster) Northern Friends Peace Board and the Friends Peace Committee, 1938. Image courtesy of Northern Friends Peace Board.)[16]

---

[16] I discovered this poster with the help of the librarians in the Quaker & Special Collections at Haverford College, where I was able to study it in full detail. This poster, depicting a mother breastfeeding her child, illustrates the way in which Quakers harnessed an intimate

Studying the testimonies of the Society of Friends women relief workers in particular as a collective independent of the male volunteers opens the way to see a pacifism instilled with an intimate ethics because, generally speaking, women on the ground in Spain were the ones forging relationships amongst the refugees and administering daily to their needs. In other words, women were often the ones setting up workshops for sewing, as Francesca Wilson did,[17] or volunteering in the hospitals, as Emily Parker did,[18] or living in the children's colonies, as Norma Jacob, with her two children, did.[19] In contrast, Alfred Jacob, the British Friends Service Council (FSC) representative who primarily oversaw the Friends' activity in Catalonia and worked relentlessly to expand their scope of aid, undertook jobs that were largely administrative, organizational, and logistical.[20] Domingo Ricart, a Spanish pacifist, worked as the "second administrator" (Mendlesohn 188) to the Barcelona unit. Richard Rees, also a male worker of the Barcelona unit, acted as their lorry driver (103). Alfred Cope, an American in the Murcia Unit, was sent to Spain mainly as a record and book-keeper (61). Many men volunteered on a short-term basis, and the male Friends who worked in fascist-held territory distributed through the Flangist local aid organization, *Auxilio Social*.[21] In a logic similar to Angela

---

ethics, an ethics of care and community, to call for an end to war and a constructive building of peace. Silhouetted behind the mother and child, a soldier firing at another soldier iterates the cycle of war-making, implying that the principle of force can either be enforced or resisted through the ideals children are taught and through the mother's support or resistance to war. The touch and care here signifies values in opposition to war—life giving opposed to life taking. Referencing a Madonna figure, this image recalls the Weeping Women of *Guernica* and the propaganda that proliferated from Spain. It can be read as commenting on the current war in Spain, or an attempted intervention in the mass mobilization of Europe and the impending Second World War. For a further reading of this poster and more considerations of how "the mother has a strong capability to create peace," see Rosie Cohen's label in the digital exhibition from Haverford College. Her arguments, edited and written collaboratively with my assistance and the students from the "Peace Testimonies in Literature & Art" Writing Seminar, have informed my thinking here.

[17] According to the Bulletin on Spanish Relief, Vol 1, No 3, pg 5 and the Oral History Interview #14 transcript pg 9.

[18] Emily Parker, in her scrapbook, has a photograph captioned: "Hospital for Children/Murcia/Here we cared for refugee children with the aid of 2 Spanish doctors, 3 English nurses, and 10 Spanish nurses."

[19] See Mendlesohn, 162.

[20] This assessment and brief description of Jacob's role is from having read the correspondence between Alfred Jacob and the Friends at Friends House, and from the information contained in Mendlesohn's book.

[21] See the appendix E labeled "Personnel" in Mendlesohn, 192. Also, for more information on the Quakers in Nationalist Spain, see Gabriel Pretus's *Humanitarian Relief Work in the Spanish Civil War*, chapter 6: "The work of the agencies (3): The America Quakers." Note, however, that what reads as Pretus's distain for the British Friends and applause of the fascist forces verges on distressing and distracting at times.

Jackson's rationale for focusing on women in her study *British Women and the Spanish Civil War*, I "seek to bring women into the historical picture" (7) of the pacifist movement during the Spanish Civil War, to refocus the picture and see what we can learn from women's perspectives and testimonies. Therefore, I argue, an analysis that puts Virginia Woolf's feminist pacifism in conversation with the women relief workers in Spain illuminates an intimate ethics that gives way to a pacifism based on personal interaction and daily activity, and traces the creation of an international peace army that could be read as a permutation of Woolf's Society of Outsiders.

Woolf outlines her ideas for the Outsiders' Society, a society dedicated to "freedom, equality, peace" (134) that works in co-operation with, but does not join, the male society for peace, throughout section III of *Three Guineas*. This political masterpiece, what Jane Marcus has called "a socialist, pacifist, and feminist polemic ("No More Horses" 267) is an attack on the structures of society that perpetuate war. Written as a series of letters to a conglomerate of societies requesting money, *Three Guineas* speculates under what conditions we can create a world in which war can be prevented. Woolf invents the Outsiders' Society, a group of women working for the causes of peace and freedom, as an essential element to this new world in which war becomes irrelevant. Woolf's Outsiders' Society would "consist of educated men's daughters working in their own class ... and by their own methods" (126) actively for the kind of positive peace already described. It is a society that is secret and pervasive, diffuse and omnipresent, and, for our purposes, most importantly, already in operation. The text contains extensive suggestions for the activities for the Society of Outsiders that can facilitate the creation of the "rights of all"[22] it seeks to protect, including, but not limited, to vow "not to fight with arms" (126); not to "make munitions or nurse the wounded" [it is important here to note that I believe Woolf to mean the wounded soldiers] (126); "to maintain an attitude of complete indifference" (127) to her brothers at war to incite him not to fight; to "bind themselves to earn their own livings" and "press for a living wage in all the professions now open to her sex; further that she must create new professions in which she can earn the right to an independent opinion" (130). It is a society that is "without office, meetings, leaders or any hierarchy, without so much as a form to be filled up, or a secretary to be paid" (135), but which has "had a positive existence for twenty years—that is since the professions

---

[22] This "rights of all" that Woolf promotes Christine Froula poignantly describes as "Woolf's modern feminism-under-erasure" (283). Froula shows Bloomsbury's civic consciousness and pacifism to be an extension of the Enlightenment project, and demonstrates how *Three Guineas*, alongside "the Gospels and Enlightenment philosophy", "advocates a critical enlargement of 'the rights of man' to encompass 'the rights of all'" (283).

were opened to the daughters of educated men" (136). Woolf offers three examples of how the Outsider's Society is already in operation; the first "an outspoken refusal to knit socks in order to discourage war," the second "an attempt to prove whether cups and awards are necessary to stimulate interest in games, and the third is an attempt to discover what happens if the daughters of educated men absent themselves from the church" (139). Here we see three different approaches to promoting the cause of peace: one, a direct protest of war; the second, an undermining of the values of competition and jealously that lead to war; and the third, a boycott of the structures and institutions that support the patriarchy, capitalism, and therefore war.

Quakers in Modernism and the Hogarth Press

God, help us to dedicate the strength we have, but seldom appreciate or use, to creating a cooperative Commonwealth where men may work together in constructive ways for their ideals.

S. Emily Parker,
From the Devotional Diary of a Relief Worker in Spain

The ideas that Woolf develops throughout *Three Guineas* concerning women's distinctive and important perspective against war, their urgent need to fight fascism by fighting patriarchy in England, and their power to disarm war-making structures through their subversive Outsiders' Society has its intellectual predecessor and counterpart in Kathleen Innes's short Quaker peace pamphlet, published in 1934, *Women and War*. Kathleen Innes was not only an active pamphleteer for the Society of Friends in London and an adamant activist for peace, she was also enmeshed in the modernist networks of the Hogarth Press.

Innes, like Virginia Woolf, maintains in *Women and War* that women have "a special point of view about war and a special contribution to make to the problem of ending it" (2). Anticipating Woolf's arguments in *Three Guineas*, Innes tells the story of a female peace worker musing "how much safer we should be... if only men would stop protecting us" (3). Compare this to Woolf's text, published four years later, when the narrative voice of *Three Guineas* addresses her "brother" who will "fight on her behalf to protect 'our' country" (128), and imagines that the Outsider will respond "'Our' country... forces me to pay others a very large sum annually to protect me, and is so little able, even so, to protect me that Air Raid precautions are written on the wall" (128). Concerned about women's position with the political advancement of

Hitler and Mussolini, Innes hits upon one of Woolf's central themes in *Three Guineas*: the connection between fascism and patriarchy, and the unstable status of women's rights in the wake of a rising fascist movement. Innes writes: "Under Fascist or Nazi Dictatorships, for example, where force is glorified, it is inevitable that the position of women should be degraded" (3). For Innes, though suffrage made strides during the Great War, the emphasis in fascist-dominated countries on the glory of violence will desecrate any of the advances made. For Woolf, this also rings true, echoing Innes's worry "Herr Hitler and Signor Mussolini have both often in very similar words expressed the opinion that 'There are two worlds in the life of the nation, the world of men and the world of women'... The emphasis which both priests and dictators place upon the necessity for two worlds is enough to prove that it is essential to their domination" (213-214n). However, Woolf also locates the romanticization of battle in the English patriarchy taking Innes's concern further, pinpointing the fascism in Germany and Italy as the same force of oppression that occurs in English fathers, the same hunger for power and control, the same disregard for other's lives, that is responsible for war: "He is called in German and Italian Führer or Duce; in our own language Tyrant or Dictator. And behind him lie ruined houses and dead bodies—men, women and children" (168). For Woolf, in order to fight the fascist in Germany, women must combat patriarchy at home and in the family, and stop supporting war-making systems worldwide.

Foreshadowing Woolf's construction of the already-existent Outsiders' Society, Innes observes in *Women and War*, "I think it is remarkable that so many Societies of women as such, have organized themselves into groups to work for Peace" (3). She proceeds to outline the great work women and women's organizations have done. Situating the women's organizations within a response to the call of intimate ethics, Innes ends her pamphlet with "What we should fear (and here I am not afraid of the appeal to fear) is the *bringing upon others* of such horror and misery as war entails, by the deliberate use of a method which is avoidable. This I find increasingly emphasized among Women's Societies and Groups" (8). For Innes, it is not the risk of being attacked that should offer the reasons for preventing war, but the danger of causing harm to the other, and, in a gesture towards intimate ethics, the Women's Societies and Groups that Innes writes about emphasize this as a central concern. From Kathleen Innes's Women's Groups and Woolf's Society of Outsiders, taken all together what we have are women operating in their communities for change, in ways that they can support, refusing to bow to the norms and standards of a system geared towards war through their direct relations with others.

These ideological junctions only begin to introduce the connections in the pacifism between Woolf and Innes, both prolific feminist pacifist writers of the modernist era. These conceptual connections between Woolf and Innes are paralleled by historical and social connections, putting one of the Society of Friends' most active pamphleteers and authors, who is now understudied and almost-forgotten,[23] in conversation with one of modernism's most significant icons. The Woolf-Innes connection displays not only the developing cultural conversation concerning a feminist pacifism, but also of the way in which the Quakers were an active, contributing part of the modernist discourse, engaging with the questions and issues of their time. If we take the example of the Hogarth Press, owned and operated by husband and wife writers and publishers Leonard and Virginia Woolf, as a microcosm of modernist production, it becomes apparent that Quaker thought and practice was shaped by and helped to shape the public discourses of the early twentieth century, through its pervasive presence in such a significant modernist network. The press, having published Sigmund Freud, T.S. Eliot, Hope Mirrlees, Nancy Cunard, H.G. Wells, Maynard Keyes, Roger Fry, Tolstoy, Chekhov, and many more iconic figures, is known as a "'site [] of production' or a 'staging venue' [] for modernism" (Southworth 12). If, indeed, as Lawrence Rainy has averred, "modernism [is] more than a series of texts or the ideas that found expression in them [but is, rather,] a social reality, a configuration of agents and practices that converge in the production, marketing, and publication of an idiom" (qtd. in Southworth 12), then Quakers are at the heart of modernism and pacifism is one of modernism's idioms. The "intersections" that the Hogarth Press, and other small presses of the era forged, "are important" Helen Southworth maintains, "because they allow one to think about cultural production as a collaborative process, outside the limits of any given text and beyond the control of any single agent" (21).[24]

---

[23] It is an unfortunate truth that a lack of materials, scholarly or otherwise, exist on Kathleen Innes. Her only known biography is a dissertation from the University of Alberta, in which her biographer, Kathryn Harvey, undertakes a feminist recuperation. This thesis comprehensively captures the extent to which "Innes *was* an international and national figure within various women's, feminist, and peace organizations, and wrote extensively about her work" (2). Harvey develops a narrative of Innes's political engagements that span from her work with the Women's International League, to the Society of Friends' Peace Committee, to her commitment to the town of her retirement.

[24] Diane F. Gillespie, in her essay "Woolfs' in Sheep's Clothing: The Hogarth Press and 'Religion'" begins the work of this task by pointing out several areas in which Quakerism, the Hogarth Press, and the Woolfs converged, though she does not develop the Society of Friends' specific thoughts or practices as one of the main religious explorations of her article, looking instead at the texts published under "Religion" in the Hogarth Catalogue. *Stories from the Old Testament*, published by Hogarth in 1920, was written by Logan Pearsall

A hinge connecting the Society of Friends to the Hogarth Press, Kathleen Innes's entrenchment and contribution to the discourses of her day illuminate the conceptual and discursive connections between the Quakers and the modernists, but also the social embeddedness of the Quakers in the causes that many famous modernists took up.[25] Innes's four books on the League of Nations published by the Hogarth Press, *The Story of the League of Nations, Told for Young People* (1925), *How the League of Nations Works, Told for Young People* (1926), *The League of Nations and the World's Workers: An Introduction to the Work of the International Labour Organization* (1927), and *The Reign of Law: A Short and Simple Introduction of the Work of the Permanent Court of International Justice* (1929), all of which were written as educational materials for children, and the collected 1936 edition *The League of Nations: The Complete Story Told for Young People*, intersect with Leonard Woolf's own interest in, and work for, the League of Nations. They also illuminate how Innes's pacifism was based in a global internationalist movement.[26] Janet M. Manson explores the way in which, "As a member of [] various organizations, particularly the Fabian Society and the League of Nations Society (LNS), which promoted the league concept, Woolf participated in crucial discussions and conferences with intellectual and political leaders to hammer out what became the British position on the League of Nations" (4). Manson then shows the extensive influence Woolf had on the

---

Smith, who was "born in America to Quaker parents" (80), as Gillespie mentions. Gillespie analyzes the way in which Pearsall Smith's *Stories* influenced Virginia Woolf's *Orlando* (82), one of Woolf's modernist masterpieces, which reinforces the connection I am making between Quakerism and modernism.

In another section of her article, Gillespie sketches Leonard Woolf's involvement with the "Questionnaire on Religious Belief," a survey that Woolf constructed and was published *The Nation and Athenaeum*. The results of writing up this "Questionnaire" were entrusted to another modernist from a Quaker background: "He [Leonard] thought R.B. Braithwaite qualified 'to interpret the results of the questionnaire', as the cover says. Braithwaite (1900-90) grew up in a Quaker family, was a pacifist who served in the Friends' Ambulance Unit during the Great War, and retained his interest of religious issues by becoming a university lecturer and then professor of moral philosophy at King's College, Cambridge" (86). Hogarth Press published these results in 1927 in a volume called *The State of Religious Belief: An Inquiry Based on 'The Nation and Athenaeum' Questionnaire* (84), again showing the convergence between Quakerism and modernism.

[25] For a further reading of Quakers and the Hogarth Press, including a study of the Press's Quaker publications and their emphasis on individual choice, social and metaphysical interconnectedness, and personal responsibility, see Foster, "Writing in the 'White Light of Truth.'"

[26] Indeed, Innes's biographer writes: "Innes joined with Helena Swanwick, Virginia Woolf, and other women to redefine 'patriotism' as a spirit compatible with that of internationalism... According to Innes, internationalism was based upon a 'sense of individual responsibility and worth' and a 'constructive effort... [to] enter into the lives of others, whether of those of another class of the same nation or of members of another nation'" (103).

British position and his emphasis on the "importance of cooperation within the international community to prevent war" (3). The internationalism that Manson writes about was a shared concern of Innes's, apparent in the pamphlets Leonard and Virginia published, and is a theme that appears as an important element in other Quaker publications of the Hogarth Press.

From Leonard and Innes's correspondence, it is clear that their networks overlapped and that they had met each other through activist channels. Leonard knew Innes under her maiden name Royds and "as former Secretary of the Women's International League."[27] It was recommended to Innes that she try Hogarth for her first children's educational text, *The Story of the League of Nations, Told for Young People*. As Secretary of the Peace Committee of the Society of Friends, Innes also collaborated with Hogarth Press for Leonard and Virginia to publish eight Quaker pamphlets based on the annual Merttens Lectures on War and Peace. [28] The Merttens Peace lectures take up the Society of Friends' historic cause of pacifism. The second lecture that Leonard and Virginia published, Francis E. Pollard's *War and Human Values* (1928), represents the internationalist spirit embodied in Kathleen Innes, and both Leonard and Virginia's writings, calling for "making the world one community instead of many" (12). This statement foreshadows the "appeal" of non-violence and precarity Butler explores in *Frames of War* and is a notion echoed in Woolf's famous feminist, socialist proclamation, "As a woman I have no country. As a woman I want no country. As a woman my country is the whole world" (*Three* 129). Taken as a collection, the internationalist threads that appear here to be ensconced in constructive pacifist philosophies become clear.

By contributing to a shared public discourse, by organizing around causes with concentric activist networks, and by engaging and debating policy and global issues, modernists and Quakers in the interwar years worked together to forge an internationalist spirit in which the flourishing of peace might be possible. It becomes apparent that Quakers and modernist public intellectuals wrote, produced, and performed in the same milieu, contributing to an engaged social conversation that fed each other's theories. When the Spanish Civil War occurred, many people who had been advocating peace in the interwar years were discouraged. However, the Society of Friends and modernists such as

---

[27] Letter from Kathleen Innes to Leonard Woolf. 1 October 1924. And Letter from Leonard Woolf to Kathleen Innes, 6 October 1924.University of Reading. MS 2750_192. Quoted with permission of The University of Sussex and The Society of Authors as the Literary Representative of the Estate of Leonard Woolf.

[28] Innes's correspondence with the press records this collaboration. See also Willis, though the Hogarth Press published eight Merttens Lectures on War and Peace and not seven, as he notes. Willis is missing mention of the 1931 publication (224).

Virginia Woolf continued to produce action and literature that supported a pacifist agenda. Jane Marcus, in her ground-breaking essay "The Niece of a Nun," which illuminates the influence that Virginia Woolf's Quaker aunt, the mystic and author Caroline Emilia Stephen, had on Woolf's feminism, muses that if it were not for the connection between patriarchy and fascism that *Three Guineas* makes, "the Outsiders' Society could be the Society of Friends" (135). Here I agree that the Society of Outsiders could not be the Society of Friends; there is not a one-to-one relation between the Society of Outsiders and the Society of Friends because the Society of Outsiders is much more pervasive and unorganized than the Society of Friends. However, when war breaks out in Spain, the Society of Friends prove to be an essential component to the Society of Outsiders, a society working against the causes of war that also includes modernists, artists, and activists from around the globe, in an attempt to spread messages and practices of peace. And it starts with an intimate ethics.

Peace Testimonies of the Spanish Civil War:
An Expression of Intimate Ethics

Farmers who have given of their crops; little children who have saved pennies; countless groups who have sent funds and materials; seamen who have braved bombs and submarines; dock-hands who have risked their lives to unload the ships; men who have transported the supplies to where we can now distribute them directly to the people. How small is our part yet how glorious to belong to a great company which knows not its many parts but which, laboring together, makes the work possible.

Emily Parker,
From the Devotional Diary of a Relief Worker in Spain

There are many versions and entrances into the matrix of the Society of Outsiders. The common theme is conducting work for peace, justice and the rights of all. These gestures are the realization of Berman's intimate ethics, I argue. As Woolf points out, some work is more active than others, and some tasks more public than others. The evolution of fascism and total war in the 1930's saw a progressive militarizing of the pacifist British left, this is true, but it also saw a spontaneous pacifist outpouring of anti-fascist activity that has, historically, not been read as pacifist, and a mobilization of peace workers, a feminist collective of outsiders, who joined together through international networks to form a web of support for the bodies under seizure in Spain.

We can trace this network starting with Virginia Woolf herself. Woolf's scrapbooks, compiled during the writing of *Three Guineas* and used as a way to document much of her source material, contain a newspaper article entitled "Democracy at Stake" (Monks House Papers (Sussex)/B16.f Vol. 2 (Sussex) 34). Listed by the General Press Cutting Association as having been printed in the *Daily Herald* on August 20, 1936, roughly one month after the outbreak of war, this article takes a stance against war in Spain, in support of the Republic, and is signed by many notable modernists, including Leonard and Virginia Woolf. Here, prominent pacifists such as Norman Angell, H.G. Wells, and the Quaker Margery Fry (also Roger Fry's sister) advocate alongside the Woolfs for "retaining belief in the British ideals of political freedom and democracy" and to express "our sympathy with the Spanish Government and people our hope that our own Government will take every legitimate opportunity of pursuing towards such a foreign Government the traditional British policy of sympathetic benevolence." Though the nationalist rhetoric here can be considered to verge on problematic, this group of writers is both expressing public support for the Republic while calling for an end to the fascist coup d'état.[29] Wanting to correct some of the proto-fascist rhetoric burgeoning in the British presses, these authors take a stand against the "attempt... being made", "particularly in the popular press... to misrepresent the nature of that struggle and to enlist the sympathies of Britain for the military rebels." We can see here how pacifist modernists are working together for a peace that is not neutral; unequivocally on the side of the Republic, this letter still calls, nevertheless, for a "policy of sympathetic benevolence" while aiming to create a popular sentiment that offers alliance with the democracy under attack.

Additionally, Jane Marcus tells us that Virginia Woolf "donated some manuscript pages of *Three Guineas*... to be sold for the aid of refugees from the Spanish Civil War" (li). As illustrated in the previous section, Leonard and Virginia both used their press to fight fascism and promote peace by publishing tracts that covered these topics.[30] Virginia Woolf wrote *Three Guineas*, which I

---

[29] Reading a *Times* printing of the same letter, Gayle Rogers points out problematic racial subtext. He writes: "a sovereign Spain is under attack by a 'junta of generals' and 'Moorish troops' under the banner of fascism... Revising some Hispanicisms, it recalls the Moorish invasions of Europe through Spain hundreds of years ago, and the letter's defense of 'British freedoms' is juxtaposed with it language of an 'invasion of Spain by an African army'" (146). The *Times* letter contains a sentence that the *Daily Mail* letter cut—it reads: "That it [the Republican government] has been able to withstand this military coup and the invasion of Spain by an African army for so many weeks has been due to the fact that it has behind it the great majority of the Spanish people of all political and religious creeds." The racialized subtext that Rogers points out is emblematic of the way in which distressing imperialist rhetoric pervaded the discourses of the modernist era, despite an attempt from many on the left to be progressive.

[30] See also Rogers, 145.

have argued elsewhere serves as her Peace Testimony.[31] I have also argued that *Three Guineas*, in and of itself, is a form of pacifist activism and a major intervention in the discourses of war.[32]

Virginia Woolf, along with Leonard and her sister, Vanessa Bell, attended the large *Spain & Culture* fundraising rally at the Royal Albert Hall on June 24, 1937, where all their names were listed for publicity of the cause on the event program. Virginia and Leonard sat on the platform behind the speakers. The image of the weeping woman on the front of the program donated by Pablo Picasso, a study for *Guernica*, is the classic figure of intimate ethics under duress. As the mother clutches the dead body of her lifeless baby, no amount of touch or care will bring the baby back. The baby, having its finitude exposed and its vulnerability exploited, no longer exists in the network of relations of ethical care, but that loss puts out an ethical call to protect the bodies and beings of others.[33]

The National Joint Committee, a conglomeration of many different aid and relief organizations, was one of the main fundraising entities in Great Britain for the Aid Spain movement,[34] and worked with many organizations like the Artists International Association (AIA), of which Vanessa Bell was a member, to raise money for Spanish relief. (It is also important to note that "Why Art Today Follows Politics," Virginia Woolf's 1936 essay, was written for the AIA and that Quentin Bell was also a member.) The AIA promoted the *"Unity of Artists for Peace, Democracy, and Cultural Development"* (Tate Archives 7043.17.3 [1938]). At the foundation of this socialist organization's mission was peace and freedom; as the war in Spain devolved, the AIA became involved in numerous fundraising missions and initiatives. The first British Artists Congress, chaired by Quentin Bell, accompanied the *Exhibition for the Unity of Artists for Peace, for Democracy, for Cultural Progress* in April and May of 1937 in which Vanessa Bell exhibited. The exhibition, reported by *The Northern Echo*,

---

[31] See "Subverting Genres and Virginia Woolf's Political Activism: *Three Guineas* as Peace Testimony."

[32] See "Writing was her fighting: *Three Guineas* as a Pacifist Response to Total War."

[33] Thanks goes to the Royal Albert Hall Archives for providing me with a copy of this program.

[34] Angela Jackson provides an overview of the contention of the field which surrounds calling the organization of Spanish relief a "movement." As she points out, "the concept of a 'movement' is of value because it is an important element in the understanding of women's perceptions of their work for Spain" and highlights "women's distinctive engagement with the public sphere" (56). Likewise, I concur that the people who organized around Spain and for Spanish relief felt themselves part of something larger and that Spain as a cause (both pacifist and militant) had the resonance and traction of a social movement. And, as this paper shows, the infrastructure dedicated to Spanish relief was certainly of a scale that constitutes a social 'movement.'

was "a demonstration by British and foreign artists of their unity in support of peace, democracy and cultural development."[35] Because Simon Martin, in his recently published *Conscience and Conflict: British Artists and the Spanish Civil War*, gives a detailed account of the AIA's Aid Spain activities, I will not give a full list here. I will, however, mention that Vanessa, Quentin, and Angelica Bell, and Duncan Grant "designed posters advertising a public meeting to raise money to send medical help to Spain" (Martin 44), which were solicited by the Spanish Medical Aid Committee (44), a subsidiary of the National Joint Committee for Spanish Relief.

The kind of efforts that were supported by Virginia Woolf and Vanessa Bell were bolstered and extended by the Society of Friends in conjunction with the Save the Children International Union. Both organizations joined forces to raise money and provide relief in Spain, were subsidiaries of the National Joint Committee,[36] and did a great deal of the distribution of goods that the National Joint Committee raised. Once artists, writers, public intellectuals, and peace activists had raised the funds in Britain, these items had to be disseminated and distributed through Spain, which women from Save the Children International and the Society of Friends worked on the ground to do.

The Quaker distribution was extensive and mobilized international support. Workers came from Britain, the United States, Denmark, and collaborated with the women in Spain and the Save the Children International Union. The International Commission for the Assistance of Child Refugees in Spain (IC), the organization of which was spearheaded by British Friend Edith Pye and came to be headed by American Friend Howard Kershner, gathered funds from twenty-four countries.[37] The relief work ran from Christmas Day, 1936, and continued after the war under Franco's reign until 1940 and then helped refugees outside of Spain for several years after.[38] Workers engaged in numerous activities, which included distribution of milk, cocoa, food, clothes; oversight and sponsorship of children's colonies; workshops for the making of goods and helping refugees to stay employed; sponsorship of indigent families; collaboration in hospitals; work on the borders giving cocoa to refugees crossing into France; distribution of bread in schools; distribution of hot meals;

---

[35] Tate Archives. TGA 901.37. Press-cuttings scrapbook page 15. Listed as "Artists Show Ideas on World Peace" *Northern Echo*, 15 April 1937.

[36] The *National Joint Committee for Spanish Relief (Booklet)* lists its "cooperating societies" as the "Social Service Council of the Society of Friends, the Save the Children Fund [the British chapter of Save the Children International Union], the Spanish Medical Aid Committee, the Scottish Ambulance Unit, the Spanish Women's Committee for Help to Spain, the Women's Committee Against War and Fascism, the Spanish Youth Foodship Committee" (2).

[37] See Kershner, *Quaker Service in Modern War*. Also see *Quaker Service in Spain*, 9.

[38] See Mendlesohn, 124, 138-139, 184.

and work in the abominable concentration camps in France in which many refugees were interned.[39] The work was recorded in September of 1938 as:

> Feeding 4,000 children in canteens in Barcelona.
> Full maintenance of 360 children in colonies in Catalonia.
> Feeding 2,000 children in Catalonia in conjunction with local authorities and International Commission.
> Support of two hospitals in Southern Spain.
> Transport and shipment of foodstuffs from England, Holland, Marseilles and U.S.A.
> Feeding and relief done in conjunction with American Friends, the Red Cross, etc (including 1,000 school children in Madrid).
> (*To My Neighbor* 3)

The pamphlet *To My Neighbor* also stresses that Friends' collaborative efforts had "provided 1.5 million hot meals" (3) in five months' time. Despite the volume of people served, the personal connection and the individual care each of the refugees (especially the children) received indicates a system of relief that recognizes, if not always succeeds at, the importance of an intimate ethics. Esther Farquhar, a representative of the American Friends Service Committee (AFSC), which worked in co-operation with the British Friends providing relief and distribution in Spain, writes of her experiences starting a canteen for infants to receive milk in Murcia. Often children required a prescription from the doctor to get milk. She reports to the American Friends:

> For three days I have sat in the doctor's office and seen him examine babies and talk to their mothers about the food that they were getting...
> Tomorrow we will give out 106 bottles to 40 babies. It's fun to watch it grow, and the mothers seem quite happy about it, and it is very satisfying to know that these babies are going to have the supervision of a very good doctor, who very evidently loves babies from the way he handles them and from the keen interest he takes in each one. He has examined 52 babies so far. If this average maintains we should be able to have at least 250 babies under the doctor's care soon and many more when the 1000 bottles come from Barcelona. (Bulletin on Spanish Relief 1.3: 4)[40]

---

[39] See *Quaker Service in Spain 1936-1940* and Hale, "Waging Peace in the Spanish Civil War."
[40] Célia Keren, in "Autobiographies of Spanish Refugee Children at the Quaker Home in la Rourviére (France, 1940)" develops the idea of a "new 'genre' of humanitarian literature" (6). With more time, and Keren's article as a background, it would be interesting to explore the way in which this "humanitarian literature" operates along the track of an intimate ethics; as

Though the relief operations affected and helped thousands of individuals, these personal interactions and stories pervade the letters and reports from the workers. Though Spain had, at one count, "2,400,000 to 3 million" (Bulletin on Spanish Relief, 27 January, 1939, 1) displaced refugees in Republican territory running from the war, those on the ground fighting the effects of the war did so one hungry mouth at a time.[41]

Being in the midst of a war-torn country made Farquhar "realize what war was and how very foolish it was" (Oral History 10) and it "convinced me more that everything that peace was something I needed to work for" (14). Work for it she did: opening milk canteens in the Murcia region, and collaborating with Francesca Wilson on establishing workshops to help refugees produce goods and stay employed. Farquhar's Oral History transcripts contain stories of the bombs and the sheer waste of life she witnessed, but they also contain reminiscences of her friendship with Francesca Wilson, and memories of bringing a group of children to a mountain retreat in the summer, to get them away from the violence. Many of her letters from Spain found their way into AFSC reports and the Bulletin on Spanish Relief Conditions, and in them we can see the way in which Farquhar held space for the personal development of individuals amidst the chaos. She witnesses the improvement of her charges, and how the children, with the help and support of the people at the colonies, were able to return to happiness:

> The most affectionate child (at the Bosque, a refugee children's colony outside Murcia) was a girl from the other side of Madrid. Her father was killed when the town was bombarded and the child was separated from her mother on the way. When she first came to Murcia she was extremely nervous and had some sort of nervous attacks frequently. She doesn't have them any more and was as happy and normal as any of them. (Bulletin 1.3: 9)[42]

Keren points out, much of this literature attempts to create a relationship with the reader, and addresses itself as an appeal (6-8).

[41] This paper focuses on the FSC and AFSC relief work in Republican territory because the nature of the relief work in fascist zones was of a different ilk. While the Quakers maintained the rights in Republican territories to engage in the direct distribution of goods, all distribution of goods in the fascist territories were conducted through the *Auxilio Social*, the local, right-wing aid organization (See Gabriel Pretus and Farah Mendlesohn, chapter 6 and chapter 4, respectively.) Also, this paper features narrative of the female relief workers in Spain, and the relief in nationalist territory was staffed almost exclusively by men (see Mendlesohn, Appendix E, 192).

[42] Keren makes apparent the difficulties that historians have encountered of gathering testimonies of the children's experiences themselves. She analyzes fifteen journals in which

Individualized care and attention to the creation of communities that support the structures of Being required for health and survival marks these relief workers' testimonies.

One of the great testimonial documents that repeatedly conveys an intimate ethics at work is a scrapbook compiled by Emily Parker held in the AFSC archives. Parker assembled pictures and memories of "eighteen months in war torn Spain." The opening of the scrapbook, intended to serve as a thank-you to all the people who donated funds to Spanish relief, declares that the book "does not attempt to portray the horrors of war but rather to show something of the constructive work in which Christian Youth in America through their contributions in cash and in kind and through their representative had a share." What follows is a pictorial record of Parker's time in Spain—photographs of children writing together, picking out books, receiving gifts of dolls. Parker includes snapshots of the cityscape of Murcia and the countryside; the women at the watering hole; groups of children posing in front of ambulances. One particularly haunting and striking image is of a tiny baby, who is sitting upright on a divan in what looks to a modern viewer like a white baptism dress. The bone-chilling caption, handwritten in blue ink, reads: "Felix—who stayed with us six months and then died. Called by the children—gato—(cat)." Interspersed throughout these photographs are women in white uniforms, relief and nursing outfits, administering to the needs of others. We see nurses holding babies, workers teaching toddlers how to walk, women passing out food and drink, volunteers posing with "their kids." From Emily Parker's collection of photographs what stands out is a Peace Testimony that relied on the attempt to recognize the individuality of the children, and to create an atmosphere in which their personalities, physical, and emotional health could thrive (even if it was not always successful) amidst the tragedies and impossible circumstances brought by the war.

Norma Jacob, one of the British Friends' representatives in Barcelona, spearheaded the Catalonia mission with her husband, Alfred Jacob. Both the Jacobs worked tirelessly to expand the scope of the Catalonia relief effort. Despite the personal exhaustion and sheer volume of people needing help, Norma still assessed individual situations and made house calls:

---

the children of the La Rourviére colony wrote about their life experiences, and locates a shared form that she speculates must have had a pedagogical methodology behind it. She does find that, though many of the children had terrible experiences of refugee shelters, once they were housed in children's colonies their situation improved (12). She also finds that we can read these journals as "palimpsest" texts, informed by layers of motivation, and though sometimes masked, the children's voices do come through the various layers (16).

Yesterday morning we had a visit from an elderly German anarchist who came to beg for milk for his little school in the slums. There were only 30 children, he said, and we couldn't possibly refuse to give them milk… he kept repeating "only thirty – you can't forget my thirty children!" We did a quick calculation and discovered that his 30 children wouldn't cost anything very exorbitant and the end of it was that I undertook to go down this morning and visit his school… I really can't tell you how those children looked – their faces were grey, with dark marks and great big eyes. The German told me that many of them were consumptive and many syphilitic….

…I am tempted to arrange to pay the 30/- a week myself…. [43]

Norma did find the funds for the thirty anarchist students, as she and her husband found funds for many indigent and hungry families in the Barcelona area. In fact, Norma continued to have a relationship with the German school teacher, and advocated for the school at every opportunity. Roughly a year later, she recounts how, "The elderly German from this school came today for the cocoa and begged also for just one piece of soap to wash the dirtiest children when they arrived at school. He was overjoyed when I gave him an exercise book and a pencil for each of his 33 children."[44]

This is just the tip of the iceberg of the vast network of relief that was mobilized against war in Spain, a network of many women who banded together under a single cause to fight the effects of total war. These women, a real-life, diffused, unofficial (for how could it be any other way?) Outsiders' Society, in my students words, "Ignited pacifism in the face of total war," by engaging an intimate ethics of care to counter the anonymous destruction wrought from battle. Woolf, through the National Joint Committee for Spanish Relief, was connected to these Outsiders, was indeed an Outsider herself advocating for the causes of peace and freedom, and through the vast *oeuvre* of her writing, as Jessica Berman shows, promoted an intimate ethics. In following the archival thread of relief work, it becomes clear that an intimate ethics is an important component of women relief workers' Peace Testimony on the ground in Spain.

---

[43] Norma Jacob to Fred Tritton. 1 November 1937. FSC/R/SP/1/3-4 Barcelona letters & reports from 1937-1938.
[44] Norma Jacob to Dorothy Thomsen. 3 September 1938. FSC/R/SP/1/3-4 Barcelona letters & reports from 1937-1938.

Bringing Pacifisms Past into the Present

> *Then events in headline form flash through my mind:*
> *Bombings in Barcelona*
> *Refugee shelters overflowing*
> *Twice-evacuated children are brought to our hospitals*
> *The raid is cut so no food may be had*
> *Bombings in Valencia*
> *Bombings in Almeria*
> *Army trucks stores in churches*
> "Were you there when they crucified my Lord?" *Yes I was!*
> *In Spain in 1938...*
> "Were you there when they crucified my Lord?" *Yes, both through the war in Spain*
> *and in a violent victory misnamed "peace."*
>
> S. Emily Parker,
> *From the Devotional Diary of a Relief Worker in Spain*

Paul Saint-Amour, in *Tense Future*, posits that we are living in a "perpetual interwar," where he uses "*inter + war* to denote not only 'between wars' but also 'in the midst of war'" (306). Violence, *Tense Future* reminds us, is not evenly distributed throughout the planet; that the simple binary of war vs. peace is a false and speciously easy division, and that "peace" is often constructed upon a violence that does not *count*, or is not recognized, as war. We can feel at "peace" while being in the midst of war. In a perpetual interwar, one is suspended, both waiting for the next war while in the midst of the present one, "the underwriting of peace in spaces conceived as central by the persistence of war in spaces conceived as peripheral" (37). Trapped as "interwar angels, blown sideways by a storm into a storm" (316), we are called to an accounting if we ever want to cease riding the winds of war.

As Americans, the blood is on our hands now. We have inherited the "perpetual interwar" guilt assumed by British bombings of Iraq in the 1920's and the bombing of Ethiopia by Italy in 1935, as the drone war in Pakistan has killed hundreds of civilians, as the war in Iraq has created tens of thousands of civilian deaths, as conflict in the Middle East and around the globe rages on. John Brenkman, though not a pacifist, proclaims outrage at America's sheer *irresponsibility:*

The denial of tragedy amounts to a denial of responsibility. Not just moral responsibility, but ultimately political responsibility. Consider the silence regarding civilian causalities in Iraq. The United States made no effort to estimate civilian deaths, or even to assist Iraqis in accounting for their dead... Our country has gone to war not wanting to know what it does. From the day of the invasion right through the destruction and depopulating of Falluja and beyond, America's leaders, its press, its representatives, its public—in short, ourselves—have indulged in this cowardly *wanting-not-to-know*. The silence is a form of lying. But the deception may be nearer self-deception than deceit. (22)

It is a form of lying to ourselves. It is, I might add, a form of perpetuating a fiction of safety, of superiority, of independence, of invulnerability, and a form of perpetuating a fiction of separation from the metaphysical and ontological ramifications of having wrought this kind of violence on another country, another person, another culture.

The network of Spanish relief, bringing these pacifisms past into our present moment, and forging a historical constellation with the thinkers, artists, writers, and peace activists here and now give us many things to consider in our work towards liberating Walter Benjamin's Angel of History from Saint-Amour's interwar storm. Our daily lives, or small actions, and the way in which we engage in discourse and treat others around us may be the greatest threat to the war-making system. War is a value that, if it can be learned, can also be unlearned. The modernist pacifists, a network in which I am including the Quakers, were operating at a pivotal moment in history, where the trajectory of war had not yet been set. Serious talks of disarmament and international co-operation for peace were underway; hope for the end of war and an intellectually viable pacifism was thought possible. These activists were establishing global pacifisms based on hope in international government, yes, but also based on the individual consciousness of the people and their power to choose peace instead of war. Virginia Woolf and the Quaker relief workers in Spain were operating in a discourse that has unveiled that a peace based on inequality and oppression is not peace; that true peace is predicated upon racial, gendered, financial, and social equality amongst people. They have opened a path for us to see that politics now, as it did then, carries with it the wail of the weeping woman, the mother who clutches her dead child—it is a primordial cry to Being itself to consider, care about, and respond to the call of the other. This response, as Leonard and Virginia Woolf, Vanessa Bell, Kathleen Innes, and the Quaker relief workers in Spain make apparent, has many expressions, but all of them are predicated on recognizing both the humanity of the other and the responsibility, as global citizens, we have to that humanity. We must mine this history, then, for pacifisms past, so that we can more clearly see the future.

Acknowledgments

This article is dedicated to Distinguished Professor Jane Marcus, whose teaching and writing has inspired much of my thought and development. I am forever in her intellectual debt.

I would also like to thank the students of the Peace Testimonies in Literature & Art Writing Seminar at Haverford College for helping me to sharpen my thinking on the motifs explored here through their class participation and diligent work on a student digital humanities and Special Collections exhibition on pacifism and social justice entitled *Testimonies in Art & Action: Igniting Pacifism in the Face of Total War*. This exhibition launched in the Fall semester of 2015 at Haverford College in the Magill Library and has contributed to my current thinking.

A shorter version of this paper was read at the twenty-fifth International Virginia Woolf Conference, *Virginia Woolf and her Female Contemporaries*, held in Bloomsburg, PA 2015.

Thank you to the archives that have helped with the research and material for this paper, especially The Library of the Religious Society of Friends in Great Britain at Friends House in London, the Archives of American Friends Service Committee in Philadelphia, the Tate Archives in London, University of Reading Special Collections, the Royal Albert Hall Archives in London, Haverford College's Quaker & Special Collections, and the University of Sussex Special Collections at The Keep in Brighton. My gratitude goes to The University of Sussex and The Society of Authors as the Literary Representative of the Estate of Leonard Woolf for permission to view and quote from the correspondence between Kathleen Innes and the Hogarth Press.

✷ Works Cited ✷

Archive Collections Consulted:
Monks House Papers University of Sussex Special Collections
University of Sussex
Brighton, England
B.16 *Three Guineas* [Kirkpatrick A23]
a. Reading notes for *Three Guineas.*
Friends Relief Work in Spain 1936-1939 Archives
Library of the Religious Society of Friends
London, England
Minutes of the Friends Service Council Spain Committee 1936-1940:
FSC/SP/M1.
FSC/R/SP/1
/1-2 Barcelona: letters and reports 1936-1937 (2 files)
/3-4 Barcelona: letters and reports from. 1937-38 (2 files)
Royal Albert Hall Archives, London, England.
Kensington Gore, London SW7 2AP, United Kingdom.
Archivist provided program from *Spain & Culture* Rally.
The Archives of the Hogarth Press
University of Reading Archives, Reading, England.
MS 2750/188 MS 2750/189 MS 2750/190 MS 2750/191 MS 2750/192 MS
2750/357 MS 2750/370 MS 2750/465
Archives of the American Friends Service Committee
Cherry Street, Philadelphia
Bulletin on Spain Relief Conditions, 1937-1939 in Publications, Newsletters,
Bulletin on Spain.
Scrapbook of S. Emily Parker in Photographs, Spain, 1938.
Oral History Interview #14. Narrator: Wilbur Kamp and Esther Farquhar
Kamp. Interviewer William Guthrie. 27 February 1989 and 20 March 1989.
Wilmington, Ohio.
Papers of the International Artists Association
Tate Archive, London, England
TGA 7043
Haverford College Quaker & Special Collections
Haverford, PA
Exhibitions:
Testimonies in Art & Action: Igniting Pacifism in the Face of Total War. Curated by J.
Ashley Foster and students from the "Peace Testimonies in Literature & Art"
Writing Seminar. Magill Library, Haverford College, Haverford, PA. 6 Oct-11
Dec 2015.

Published Material:

Berman, Jessica. *Modernist Commitments: Ethics, Politics, and Transnational Modernism*. New York: Columbia University Press, 2012. Print.

Brenkman, John. *The Cultural Contradictions of Democracy: Political Thought since September 11*. Princeton: Princeton University Press: 2007. Print.

Brockington, Grace. *Above the Battlefield: Modernism and the Peace Movement in Britain, 1900-1918*. New Haven: Yale University Press, 2010. Print.

Brown, Runham H. *Spain: A Challenge to Pacifism*. London: The Finsbury Press, 1937. Print.

Butler, Judith. *Frames of War: When is Life Grievable?* London and New York: Verso, 2010. Print.

---. *Giving an Account of Oneself*. New York: Fordham University Press, 2005. Print.

Cole, Sarah. *At the Violet Hour: Modernism and Violence in England and Ireland*. Oxford and New York: Oxford University Press, 2012. Print.

Cunard, Nancy, ed. *Authors Take Sides on the Spanish Civil War*. London: Left Review, 1937. Print.

Dandelion, Pink. *An Introduction to Quakerism*. New York: Cambridge University Press, 2007. Print.

Froula, Christine. *Virginia Woolf and the Bloomsbury Avant-Garde*. New York: Columbia University Press, 2004. Print.

Foster, J. Ashley. "Writing in the 'White Light of Truth': History, Ethics, and Community in *Between the Acts*." *Woolf Studies Annual* 22 (2016). [Forthcoming.]

---."Writing Was Her Fighting: Three Guineas as a Pacifist Response to Total War." *Critical Insights: Virginia Woolf & 20th Century Women Writers*. Ed. by Kathryn Stelmach Artuso. Ipswitch: Salem Press, 2014: 54-74. Print.

---. "Subverting Genres and Virginia Woolf's Political Activism: Three Guineas as Peace Testimony." *The Virginia Woolf Miscellany*. Ed. by Emily Kopley & Sarah Sullam. Special edition: "Virginia Woolf and Literary Genres." 83 (Spring 2013): 20-22. Print.

Gillespie, Diane F. "'Woolfs' in Sheep's Clothing: the Hogarth Press and 'Religion'." *Leonard & Virginia Woolf, The Hogarth Press, and the Networks of Modernism*. Ed by Helen Southworth. Edinburgh: Edinburg University Press, 2010: 74-99. Print.

Give For Spain; [an appeal]. Friends Service Council. London: Friends House, 1937. Print.

Graham, Helen. *The War and Its Shadow: Spain's Civil War in Europe's Long Twentieth Century*. Brighton: Sussex University Press, 2012. Print.

---. *The Spanish Civil War: A Very Short Introduction*. Oxford and New York: Oxford University Press, 2005. Print.

Hale, F. "Waging Peace in the Spanish Civil War: The Relief Efforts of the British Quaker Mission." *Studia Historiae Ecclesiasticae*. 31. 2 (October 2005): 445-470. Print.

Historical Dictionary of the Friends (Quakers), 2nd ed. Ed. Margery Post Abbott, Mary Ellen Chijioke, Pink Dandelion, and John William Oliver Jr. Lanham, MD: The Scarecrow Press, 2012. Print.

Harvey, Kathryn. *"Driven by War into Politics!": A Feminist Biography of Kathleen Innes.* A thesis submitted to the Faculty of Graduate Studies and Research in partial fulfillment of the requirements for the degree of Doctor of Philosophy. Edmonton: University of Alberta, 1995. Online PDF. Accessed 15 May 2015.

Innes, Kathleen E. *Women and War.* London: Friend's Peace Committee, 1934. Print.

---. *The Story of the League of Nations: Told for Young People.* London: Hogarth Press, 1925. Print.

---. *How the League of Nations Works, Told for Young People.* London: Hogarth Press, 1926. Print.

---. *The League of Nations and the World's Workers: An Introduction to the Work of the International Labour Organization.* London: Hogarth Press, 1927. Print.

---. *The Reign of Law: A Short and Simple Introduction of the Work of the Permanent Court of International Justice.* London: Hogarth Press, 1929. Print.

---. *The League of Nations: The Complete Story Told for Young People.* London: Hogarth Press, 1936. Print.

---. *The Prevention of War.* London: Friends Peace Committee, 1932. Print.

Jackson, Angela. *British Women and the Spanish Civil War.* London: Rutledge, 2002. Print.

Keren, Célia. "Autobiographies of Spanish Refugee Children at the Quaker Home in La Rouviére (France, 1940): Humanitarian Communication and Children's Writings." *Les Cahiers de Framespa,* 5 (2010). Provided by the Archives of the AFSC. Print.

Kershner, Howard Eldred. *Quaker Service in Modern War.* New York (?): Prentice Hall, 1950. Print.

Manson, Janet M. "Leonard Woolf as an Architect for the League of Nations." *The South Carolina Review,* Clemson University Press, 2007. On Clemson University Press Virginia Woolf International Selected Papers. Online PDF. Accessed 1 August, 2015.

Marcus, Jane. "The Niece of a Nun: Virginia Woolf, Caroline Stephen, and the Cloistered Imagination." *Virginia Woolf and the Languages of Patriarchy.* Bloomington: Indiana University Press, 1987. 115- 135. Print.

---. Introduction. *Three Guineas,* by Virginia Woolf. Orlando: Harcourt, 2006. Print.

---. "No More Horses." *Women's Studies* 4 (1977): 265-290. Print.

Martin, Simon. *Conscience and Conflict: British Artists and the Spanish Civil War.* Farnham and Burlington: Lund Humphries, 2014. Print.

Mendlesohn, Farah. *Quaker Relief Work in the Spanish Civil War.* Lamenter and Lewiston: Edwin Mellen Press, 2002. Print.

Mills, Jean. *Virginia Woolf, Jane Ellen Harrison, and the Spirit of Modernist Classicism.* Columbus: Ohio State University Press, 2014. Print.

National Joint Committee on Spanish Relief (Booklet). Warwick Digital Collections: Archives of the Trade Unions Congress. Reference number 292/946/18b/26. Online. Accessed 1 August 2015.

Parker, S. Emily. *From the Devotional Diary of a Relief Worker in Spain*. Np. Haverford Quaker & Special Collections. BX 7705 S8 P24. Print.

Pollard, Francis E. *War and Human Values*. Mertons Lectures on War & Peace No 2. London: Hogarth Press, 1928. Print.

Patterson, Ian. *Guernica and Total War*. London: Profile Books, 2007. Print.

Preston, Paul. *The Spanish Civil War: Reaction, Revolution, and Revenge*. New York and London: W.W. Norton and Co, 2006. Print.

Pretus, Gabriel. *Humanitarian Relief in the Spanish Civil War 1936-1939*. Lampeter: Edwin Mellen, 2013. Print.

Quaker Service in Spain 1936-1940. London: Friends Service Council, 1941. Print.

Robeson, Paul. "The Artist Must Take Sides." *Paul Robeson Speaks*. Secaucus: Citadel Press, 1978. 118-119. Print.

Rogers, Gayle. *Modernism and the New Spain: Britain, Cosmopolitan Europe, and Literary History*. Oxford: Oxford University Press, 2013. Print.

Saint-Amour, Paul K. *Tense Future: Modernism, Total War, Encyclopedic Form*. Oxford and New York: Oxford University Press, 2015. Print.

Southworth, Helen. "Introduction." *Leonard & Virginia Woolf, The Hogarth Press, and the Networks of Modernism*. Ed. by Helen Southworth. Edinburgh: Edinburg University Press, 2010: 1-26. Print.

Stephen, Caroline Emelia. *Light Arising: Thoughts on the Central Radiance*. Cambridge: W. Heffer & Sons; London: Headley Bros, 1908. Print.

To My Neighbor. Friends Service Council. London: Friends House, 1938. Print.

"The Vortex in Spain: To the Editor." *The Times* (London, England). 19 August 1936: 6.

Weinthraub, Stanley. *The Last Great Cause: Intellectuals and the Spanish Civil War*. New York: Weybright and Tally, 1968. Print.

Willis, J.H., Jr. *Leonard and Virginia Woolf as Publishers: The Hogarth Press, 1917-1941*. Charlotte and London: University Press of Virginia, 1992. Print.

Woolf, Leonard. *The Framework of a Lasting Peace*. New York and London: Garland Publishing, 1971. Print.

Woolf, Virginia. *Three Guineas*. Ed by Jane Marcus. Orlando: Harcourt, 2006. Print.

---. "Why Art Today Follows Politics." *Selected Essays*. Ed by David Bradshaw. Oxford: Oxford University Press, 2008: 213-215.

---. "Thoughts on Peace in an Air Raid." *Selected Essays*. Ed by David Bradshaw. Oxford: Oxford University Press, 2008: 216-219.

✳ 4 | Quaker Literature: Is There Such a Thing? ✳

Quakers and fiction:
Towards breaking out of the backward gaze

by Diane Reynolds

Only such writings as spring from a living experience will reach the life in others, only those which embody genuine thought in clear and effective form will minister to the needs of the human mind. A faith like Quakerism should find expression in creative writing born of imagination and spirit.

London Yearly Meeting, 1925

quoted from *Imagination and Spirit*, Ed. J. Brent Bill

Quakers have received Nobel prizes in science and peace, and have produced world class non-fiction: the journals of John Woolman and George Fox, and Thomas Kelly's *Testament of Devotion* reach an audience far beyond Friends. A distinctive written Quaker voice arguably exists in the stream of its expository narrative. This voice emerges from a passionate center, as writers groping within the confines of language attempt to describe and articulate often difficult and painful spiritual experiences rooted in historical reality: the English Civil War, American slavery, Nazism.

Friends have not developed a similar stream in prose fiction, opting instead for a form of writing characterized by a domesticating and often nostalgic Quakerism. This leads to two queries: What could create a Quaker literature as powerful as the best Quaker expository prose and why is this important?

Some will argue that the early Quaker rejection of fiction explains the lack of a world-class fiction—and this is not wrong. But for the last century or more, as Friends have embraced the arts, the quality of our fiction has continued to lag. This essay will first look at works by Jessamyn West, Elfrida Vipont Foulds and James Michener, chosen because Curtis and Bill's anthology of Friends' fiction, *Imagination and Spirit* excerpts them as representative Quaker writings. By comparing these excerpts to Kelly's *Testament of Devotion* and poetry by Quaker Helen Morgan Brooks, this essay will attempt to outline some of Quaker fiction's limitations and reflect on ways of transcending these limitations that might help us more fully imagine ourselves as a Society.

I proceed too with the understanding that while it may be unfair to compare literature written with different purposes for different audiences, I do this not to disparage Quaker fiction, but to illuminate larger issues. Using a model Jim Hood borrows from theorists John Guillory and Geoffrey Harpham, I will argue that much Quaker fiction (short stories and novels) has fallen into the realm of the "moral," while the best Quaker poetry and non-fiction falls into the category of the "ethical."

If we define morality as a largely black and white choice between two clear alternatives, we see that it can become "a prescriptive determination between right and wrong ... an algorithm." This contrasts to ethics, "a genuine dilemma, any outcome of which will produce positives and negatives" (Hood 119). Ethical dilemmas don't have clear-cut answers and may offer us no "good" alternatives, only choices between morally compromised options, such as when the protagonist in William Styron's novel *Sophie's Choice,* arriving at a concentration camp, must pick one of her two children to live or face having both killed (Hood 119). Within such an ethical frame, we are invited to engage in thinking about problems that don't have clear answers and thus we can attain "a fuller humanity." John Keats's vision of negative capability offers an additional resource for understanding this definition of ethics by locating a model for ethical practice in getting one's own ego out of the way and developing "a deepening regard for the claims of the other" (Hood 118).

Moral Quaker fictions

Jessamyn West's *The Friendly Persuasion* opens with "Music on the Muscatatuck." In this story, Quaker Jess Birdwell travels from Indiana to Philadelphia. While there, the music-loving Jess succumbs to a jovial salesman and purchases an organ. This causes a conflict: Jess's beloved organ clashes with Quaker prohibitions against music, so Jess "hides" the organ in his attic. When a group of elders come to call, presumably to investigate rumors about the instrument, his daughter, Mattie, not knowing what is going on below, begins to play. In a comic scene, Jess prays louder and longer, longer and louder, trying unsuccessfully to drown out the music.

In this lighthearted story, we, as an audience identify with Jess being torn between his meeting and his music, and with the humanity he shows in his love for a forbidden organ, with all its sexual undertones suggesting a person trying to break out of a potentially emasculating culture and into potency.

Jess's world, however, doesn't require confronting serious problems or making hard choices. He violates a Quaker "rule," but there's no sacrifice or real pain involved. The elders smile and look the other way about the organ, the family livelihood isn't threatened by the purchase, and while Jess's wife, Eliza, a Quaker minister, initially puts up a protest, she quickly acquiesces to the change.

Eliza has "a mind of her own" (3) but we quickly understand how domesticated that mind is—and lest Eliza be perceived as a threat, we receive a lesson in how women—even woman ministers—should behave. When Eliza sees the organ, this woman with "a mind of her own" immediately worries "what's the neighbors to think? What's the Grove Meeting to think?" (12) Following that, she delivers an ultimatum: it's the organ or her. At this point, West slips in a homily about female behavior:

> Jess had a heart as soft as pudding, and if Eliza'd said Please, if she'd let a tear slip out of her soft black eye, that organ would have been done for; but commands, threats, that was a different matter entirely … the pudding froze and if you weren't careful you'd find yourself cut to the bone on an ice splinter. (12)

Jess moves ahead with his plan, so Eliza sits down in the snow until she's soaked through and, after Jess ignores her as if she is a pouting child, she decides to give in for the sake of "peace." As a "compromise," Jess agrees to house the organ permanently in the attic.

Such anecdotes serve to normalize Quakerism within the context of mid-20th century white middle class culture. Quakerism functions here as quaint window dressing—safe and evocative of a simpler, more pastoral past. West spends a good deal of time describing the bounteous Birdwell farm: "the best stock of berries and fruits west of Philadelphia …pears, currants, gooseberries, whatever the land could support or fancy demand …" (3). Quakerism is a faith full of "theeing" and" thouing," praying, and kindhearted people with peculiar religious practices ([supposedly] no music, [safe] female preachers, a few Quaker books on the shelf) but which really differs little from other faiths. Nothing in the story challenges us to transformation because any concept of Quakerism as radically other is alien to West's project.

The Birdwell farm in this story even appears to run without actual labor. The fish jump out of the river: "Catfish … would come out of the water with their jaws clamped about a piece of cotton batting" (4). We don't see people working —the farm seems to run itself. Even the organ—described as a fairly massive instrument—seems to magically transport itself to the attic. Fantasy might be a better word for the land where the fish jump onto the hooks, nobody labors and Quaker values are reduced to winking at organ music. West depicts infantile behavior (pouting in the snow) in a "female preacher" without blinking an eye, and even suggests that this preacher engage in female wiles and manipulations to manage her "man." As Raymond Williams writes of seventeenth-century country house poems in *The Country and the City*, in West's type of pastoral fantasy, "all things come naturally to man, for his use and enjoyment, and without his effort" (31). Thomas Carew's view of nature, in the seventeenth-century poem "To Saxham," is strikingly similar to West's obliging catfish:

> every beast, himself did bring,
> Himself to be an offering.
> The scalie herd, more pleasure took
> Bath'd in the dish than in the brook. (Williams 29)

Although set in a more urban English environment, Elfrida Vipont Foulds' "A Ridiculous Idea" also normalizes Quaker ideology. In this story the main character, Kit, faces a conflict: Whether or not to delay music school to become "Father's secretary" (85). (Kit and her best friend "Pony" both have the names of harmless domesticated animals.) Although Kit says music "is the one thing I really want to do" (92), when the adults in her life tell her to become a secretary, she acquiesces with hardly a protest. She fears anything else might upset her father, who may (or may not) have a heart condition. Her own needs and leadings are ignored—except to the extent that she's pacified by being offered what she can fit around the crevices, such as borrowing music from the "Music Library" (93) in town—and in the end, she's so identified with the adults closest to her that she gets angry at her music teacher for being upset at her choice. Here, the reader learns to follow the model of sacrificing one's selfhood to the needs of a more powerful figure. The story never questions whether this kind of "getting along" and "not rocking the boat" might be antithetical to the Quaker tradition of speaking truth to power and following one's leadings even if they fly in the face of convention.

In James Michener's novel *Chesapeake*, Puritans punish a fictional Quaker, Thomas Kenworthy: "By the twenty-fifth lash, Thomas Kenworthy was nearly dead, but now the governor directed that the whip be turned over to a new aspirant eager to show how well he could strike, and pieces of flesh flicked off the bloody mass" (196). Here, Michener reduces both Kenworthy and his Puritan enemies to caricatures: Kenworthy is a holy, blameless saint and martyr, who unlike real Quakers, does not suffer. "We are children of God," he says, "and returning to him can never be painful." We're also told "he was living in a kind of ecstasy in which whippings and gibbets were no longer of much concern" (167). In turn, the Puritans are unabashed sadists who openly approve the violence inflicted on Kenworthy.

This kind of twentieth-century Quaker prose fiction does not represent the prophetic Quaker voice that has traditionally challenged power and called people to a radical re-understanding of their relationship with God.

Ethical writing

Kelly's *A Testament of Devotion*, written and published at almost the same time as *The Friendly Persuasion*, represents part of a stream that includes Robert Barclay, who wrote in *The Apology*: "He that comes to build a new city, must first remove the old rubbish, before he can see to lay a new foundation; and he that comes to an house greatly polluted and full of dirt, will first sweep away and remove the filth, before he puts up his own good and new furniture" (120). Three hundred years later, Kelly observes of holy obedience: "it is a life and power that can break forth in this tottering Western culture and return the church to its rightful life as a fellowship of creative, heaven-led souls" (29). In both, we hear the language of challenge and a call to transformation.

In contrast to Muscatatuck, Kelly's "Holy Obedience" reflects a struggle with life, death, and eternity. Kelly, not long home from a trip to Nazi Germany, during which he was haunted by the conditions under which

Quakers endured, wrote to his wife of his experience, "Until you have lived in this world of despair and fear and abysmal suffering of the soul, you can never know [how it feels]" (qtd. in R. Kelly 97) In Cologne's cathedral, Kelly's face-to-face with heart of darkness led to his being "melted down by the love of God" (T. Kelly 120). His essay thus implores us, passionately, to transcend the mediocrity of the kind of bland religiosity described in Muscatatuck: "Out in front of us is the drama of men and nations, seething, struggling, laboring, dying. Upon this tragic drama in these days our eyes are all set with anxious watchfulness and in prayer" (25). How we practice our religious faith involves the very fate of history itself. Kelly writes: "I mean this literally, utterly, completely, and I mean it for you and for me—commit yourself in unreserved obedience to Him" (26). Kelly calls this proposal "revolutionary." "Obey now," he prods (33). Nothing of half measures. As if answering back to the world of Muscatatuck he writes: "This is something different from mild, conventional religion ... against whose ... passionlessness George Fox and his followers flung themselves with all the passion of a glorious and a new discovery" (27). This is not the enameled world of the pastoral where the fish jump out of the stream in their eagerness to be served on the dinner platter. If West celebrates conformity, Kelly argues that the world needs nothing less than a rupture with the past. This life he envisions—and he would die with *Testament of Devotion* in a raw, unfinished form—is "breath-taking," "astonishing," "cruciform and blood stained," "amazing," "God-intoxicated." It discomforts us in our complacency, decenters us, and tries to pry our fingers from the security of Muscatatuck. Kelly attempts to see the world in a radically othered way.

West and Kelly offer different responses to the social turmoil of the 1930s. West provides a zone of safety, a place of refuge from reality, a backward-looking and normalizing reassurance against fear and uncertainty. Kelly, in contrast, challenges us to embrace the radical change that transforms the world into the Kingdom of God.

I would argue that "Holy Obedience," in its juxtaposition of Christian mysticism with a stripping down of religious externals to the bare essentials of a confrontation with obedience, arises from a Quaker understanding of the divine. There's a voice—experiential, visionary, immediate, all consuming and unflinching—a cry of mysticism unweighted by liturgy or a complicated edifice of theology, ripping the veil that separates humans from the eternal. Achieving a similar voice and depth in Quaker fiction is a goal yet to be achieved.

The work of poet Helen Morgan Brooks (1904-89) speaks from the perspective of the marginalized and also offers a way forward to an articulation of a Quaker experience that critiques and spills beyond the boundaries of white middle-class cultural norms. Her poetry—the following quotes come from her poems gathered into the anthology *Black Fire*—looks at the lives of the subaltern, where all is not pastoral or sweet. In "Slum House," "rats scream and roaches crawl, and the smell of urine is on the floor" (10-11). Depicting faith as the cry of a suffering humanity rather than a quaint, antiquarian artifact, in "Revelation" Brooks calls for God's mercy on "all little people, all hopeless ones ... the whoremongers, the parasitical ... the mentally deficient, the degraded ... the sick, the weak" (3-13).

In "Double Chain," Brooks urges readers truly to look at the often invisible black woman: "If you see a black queen's grace, a slattern or a wench ... try to conjure from your mind the will and soul to learn this strange alchemy of her race" (2-6). She then locates the redemptive story of God's grace among broken places and people. In "The Bus Comes," she writes, "I must believe in love/As a testimony against madness/and war and broken promises" (41-43). Also in "The Bus Comes," Brooks rejects sanitizing love's pain as she looks at love and death:

> Love is the fragrance
> that lingers around the altar rail,
> After the lilies and the carnations
> have been taken out/to lie beside the new coffin. (19-23)

Rather than try to impose a normalizing morality on us, Brooks invites us into a world of ugliness and beauty, cruelty and grace, pain and love, not a false, enamel word where pain has been removed, but a real world in which God moves among the suffering.

Without imagination, the people perish

A glance at post-1850 and particularly post-Civil War U.S. Quaker book and article titles—these are not necessarily written by Quakers but represent a back-and-forth in which positive outsider images were internalized by Friends—suggests that Quakerism came to reflect a nostalgia for a "purer," more rural ethos before the influx of non-Northern European immigrants that coincided with industrialization and the growth of urban centers. Titles include *Edith, or the Quaker's daughter: A Tale of Puritan Times* and "The Quaker of Olden Time." These works, which appear to attempt to identify Quakers with the establishment of an American morality rooted in English heritage, have perhaps too little negative capability and too much ego gratification in identifying Quakers with the "Good." The self-emptying or negative capability of Quakers found in often searing personal self-examination here turns reflexively to a protectiveness and ego-identification with the group that makes it difficult for us to describe Quakers in the aggregate as anything but the "pure lilies" of Charles Lamb's memory in *Essays of Elia*: "The very garments of a Quaker seem incapable of receiving a soil; and cleanliness in them to be something more than the absence of its contrary. Every Quakeress is a lily …."[1]

Our fiction perhaps continues to have to do with maintaining this hedge.

If we gaze into the mirror that celebrates Quakers as a pristine group apart, we may learn something about ourselves and our shrinking numbers. If our non-fiction and poetry reflect individuals' soul searching and confrontation with the darkness both within ourselves and the larger society, our fictions, in contrast, have presented us a group—a Society—to the outer world as rural, nostalgic and non-threatening: happy, benign and innocent, a fictional canon that has excised Job and Judges, that jumps from Jesus healing to Jesus resurrected, but skips the hard parts in between. This is as true of liberal Quakers as of conservative: how many times have liberal Quakers rejected the Bible for its violence, gore and horror, positing Quakers as somehow better than that? (Molly Gloss's Hugo award nominated *The Dazzle of Day* perhaps exemplifies the liberal Quaker- collective-as-Good meme.) How can our messy reality fail to disappoint newcomers who expect an ethereal New Jerusalem— or at least the triumph of "beyond consensus" within our walls?

This brings us back to Keats and his "Ode on a Grecian Urn," a poem which on one level presents the dilemma between a static but beautiful art, freezing a moment of joyful youth but never allowing the joy to be fulfilled, against the implicit reality of aging, bruising, hurting, dying and the continuous rebirth inherent in life. And it brings us Oscar Wilde's *The Picture of Dorian Gray*, in which a young man trades his soul for eternal youth. Have we, in Quaker fiction, opted to trade our collective soul for an image, our growth for a static, if beautiful, picture on a vase?

Rather than hide behind a backward-looking hedge, an ethical Quaker literature might confront the real issues contemporary Quakers face: our own struggles with and capitulations to the military industrial complex and global power structures that use our money and resources to fund projects, such as

---

[1] "A Quakers' Meeting," 53. While Quakerism, and especially Quaker "plainness" came to be increasingly associated with outward cleanliness—see for example, H.J. Clayton's 1883 *Clayton's Quaker Cookbook*, which extols Quaker butter for coming from supposedly cleaner Quaker spring houses—Lamb may be covertly expressing some of his earlier (and later submerged) radicalism in his comments on Quakers, but the point here is how such statements tended over time to replace earlier interior purity with outward appearance.

wars, hard and soft, antithetical to our Quaker witness. An ethical literature might practice negative capability, jettisoning the collective ego that longs to project Quakers as purer than other faith groups in favor of a hard look at our complacency and often easy lives in the midst of growing crisis. Such a literature might even attract people—as Dostoevsky's relentlessly dark Catholicism spoke truth to seekers like Dorothy Day—to join our group not because of our supposed perfections, but because of our honest struggles with our own—and humanity's—flaws.

✻ Works Cited ✻

Barclay, Robert. *The True Christian Divinity, as Set Forth in Eight Propositions of R. Barclay's Apology*. London: The British Library, 1817. Web. 28 May 2015.

Brooks, Helen Morgan. "Double Chain," "Revelation," "Slum House" in *Black Fire: African American Quakers on Spirituality and Human Rights*. Eds. Hal Weaver, Paul Kriese, and Steve Angell. Philadelphia: QuakerPress, 2012. Print.

Brooks, Helen Morgan. "The Bus Comes," quoted in Schaefer, Madeline. "The Bus Comes." *Acting in Faith: Connecting Friends to the work of AFSC*. N.p., 14 Feb. 2014. Web. 28 May 2015.

Bill, J. Brent, ed. *Imagination & Spirit: A Contemporary Quaker Reader*. Richmond, Ind: Friends United Press, 2003. Print.

Edith Or The Quaker's Daughter: A Tale Of Puritan Times (1856). Whitefish, Mt.: Kessinger Publishing, 2010. Web.

Foulds, Elfrida Vipont "A Ridiculous Idea." *Imagination & Spirit: A Contemporary Quaker Reader*, Eds. C. Michael Curtis, J. Brent Bill. Richmond, Ind: Friends United Press, 2003. 81-97. Print.

Gloss, Molly. *The Dazzle of Day*. New York: Tor Books, 1998. Print.

Hood, Jim. "Keats and Ethical Practice." Eds. Donn Weinholtz, Jeffrey Dudiak, and Donald A. Smith. *Quaker Perspectives in Higher Education*. San Bernadino: Full Media Services, 2014. 117-126. Print.

Keats, John. "Ode on a Grecian Urn." *The Poems of John Keats*. Ed. Jack Stillinger. Cambridge: Harvard UP, 1978. Print.

Kelly, Richard M. *Thomas Kelly: A Biography*. New York: Harper & Row, 1966. Print.

Kelly, Thomas R. *A Testament of Devotion*. Reprint edition. San Francisco: HarperOne, 1996. Print.

Lamb, Charles. "The Quakers' Meeting." *Essays of Elia*. Baudry's European Library, 1835. 49-53. Print.

Michener, James A. *Chesapeake*. 1st edition. New York: Random House, 1978. Print.

"The Quaker of Olden Time." *Living Age* 9.133 (2 May 1846): 225.

West, Jessamyn. *The Friendly Persuasion*. New York: Harcourt, Brace and Company, 1940. Print.

Wilde, Oscar. *The Picture of Dorian Gray*. 1891. London & New York: Penguin Books, 2003. Print.

Williams, Raymond. *The Country and the City*. New York: Oxford University Press, 1975. Print.

Going Naked as a Sign:
Quaker Utopianism and the Alien Other in
Joan Slonczewski's *A Door Into Ocean*

by Edward F. Higgins

Notions of utopianism are, of course, a mainstay of science fiction literature, though generally weighted heavily toward dystopian, or anti-utopian, themes. One of my favorite dystopian stories of this sort is also billed as the world's shortest science fiction story. Forrest J Ackerman has a story titled "Cosmic Report Card Earth." Its brief, one letter entirety reads simply: "F" (Heintz 234). Within its terse cleverness resides the full didactic bite and jeremiad warning of all utopian/dystopian science fiction. That cosmic "F" appraises and indicts our real world text beyond Ackerman's enstoried one. We are the adjudged children of the cosmic classroom. But hang on to this report card for a bit, I'll return to it later.

My own cosmic assessment here will concentrate on the thematic interplay between Quaker-informed ideology and the alien other as utopian tension in Joan Slonczewski's second novel, her 1986 award-winning *A Door Into Ocean*. Slonczewski's novels generally are grounded in Quaker values reflecting that group's historic moral-ethical ethos of non-violence, gender equality, and idiosyncratic spirituality, thus making informed Quakerism a useful element of interpretation. Asked about the importance of Quakerism to her fiction, Slonczewski has replied it forms the "central focus" of her early books (Levy 14). And further as she notes:

My experience with the Quakers permeates everything I write. I have been shaped by the Quaker example of listening and relating to that of God in everyone and every creature. In my books, wherever people resolve differences by intersecting seemingly irreconcilable views that comes directly out of what I've seen among Quakers. (Qtd. in Schellenberg and Switzer 5)

A Door Into Ocean is frequently cited as a feminist utopian parable. Undeniably Slonczewski is a feminist SF writer, yet her novel's underlying thematic ideology remains very much Quaker-based utopian in its moral-ethical and spiritual imperatives, even when these are reflective of particular feminist concerns. Transformatively veiled, *A Door Into Ocean* appropriates Quaker typologies as central story elements in the lives of her all-female aliens who practice an eco-stewardship, Quaker-like governance, and a spirituality on their sea-covered moon world that has allowed them to peacefully prosper for eons past their apparently long-ago separation from genetically compatible human ancestors. Peacefully prosper, that is, until the coming of the nearby planet Valedon's traders, who although initially welcomed as human sisters have cast serious doubt on their humanity through their destructive actions.

An intriguing emblem throughout the novel is that the women of Shora go unclothed, in all their amethyst-skinned glory. Not that this is a particularly erotic nudity, although Sharers, as they call themselves, are clearly sexual in their same-sex society. After generations of male-less breeding by mechanical ova-merging, anatomical differences no longer enable heterosexual coupling. For these fundamentally water-adapted humans on a temperate world, clothing holds no practical value—in fact it seems a bit foolish, if not suspect, to them. Symbolically there's an obvious Edenic-utopian resonance here. Slonczewski's Sharers are innocently naked and unashamed. Furthermore, an unassuming straightforwardness is emblemized: Sharers have nothing to hide physically and are likewise guileless in their dealings with outsiders. By contrast, the novel's clothed Valedon protagonists emblemize all that is cloaked outwardly in guises of patriarchal power with its hierarchical rankings, duplicities, and oppressions. The "soldier's plumage" of invading troops is an especially contrastive symbol to the naked and seemingly defenseless amethyst women. Soldiers engage in "share-killing"—a human action unknown to Shorans except as a rare pathology. These outwardly-appareled off-world soldiers, in alarming militarist rigidity, are seen as muting if not actually confirming an underlying lack of humanity.

Disconcerting nakedness offers an interesting historical Quaker analog. To the consternation of their contemporaries, early Quakers practiced a kind of turbulent witnessing they called "going naked as a sign." This symbolic communication was an extreme public enactment of founder George Fox's exhortation to "let your lives speak" (191). Challenging conventional norms and to attract attention to their message, individuals or small groups would sometimes go naked as an iconic sign of prophetic warning for others to repent or reform their ways. These Friends would appear in a public street, marketplace, or religious gathering shockingly unclad or arrayed in scant sackcloth thereby enacting a visual metaphor of their verbal message. Such naked semiotic truth, however, was generally ill received as "heathenish" and "shameless" by their seventeenth-century English audience, and roundly maltreated even when understood as shock-effect parable. The practice eventually declined as a counterproductive message-carrying device (although the Woodstock generation's secular revival of this method, as well as the academy awards presentation, attests to its still palpable effectiveness in speaking against conventional norms) (Bauman 92-93).

Slonczewski's Sharers employ "witnessers" in much the same way early Quakers saw moral enactment as empowered reproof. Central to Quaker belief is the notion that all human beings can be responsive to Truth because of a universalizing Inward Light in each person. Friends were admonished to "answer that of God in every one," indicating both motive for action and that which calls forth in others an acknowledgment of divine Light in themselves (Childress 18). Through this central linking theme, Slonczewski's alien Sharers confront their Valon invaders and seek to answer their presumed soul-deep humanness. Of course, answering that of God in others isn't necessarily a matter of easy course or successful endeavor.

Early on in the story, exploratory teams leave their Ocean moon to investigate the nearby planet Valedon so they might "share a fair judgment of Valan humanness." Slonczewski quickly establishes the novel's utopian/dystopian tensions around contrasting Valedon-Shora values and worldviews. We follow two main Sharer characters, Merwen and her lovesharer mate, a scientist-healer named Usha, in their information-gathering visit. They encounter a host of contrasting elements between the two cultures. Alarming poverty, violence, stratified social disharmony, and an exploitative materialist economy overshadowed by a ruling feudalistic patriarchy mar Valan life. Despite their contrary, destructive behaviors on Shora and toward Shorans— whom most Valans view contemptuously as "catfish" and treat as sub-human—can Valans indeed be human themselves? "Truth is a tangled skein. . ." (15) as Merwen notes to an eighteen-year-old male Valan who, facing few prospects on his own world, returns with them to Shora under Merwen's sponsorship and tutelage. Spinel will be a last hope test in her attempts to determine for her sisters if this dry-world species might after all be human themselves.

Sharers govern themselves through the Gathering, patterned on historic Quaker Meeting, especially the Quaker Meeting for Business. A common misunderstanding of Quaker governance is that it is based on consensus. Instead, Quakers seek a Spirit-guided Unity around whatever issues or "concerns" arise. Despite even sometimes-contentious dispute, Friends seek to discern divine will, in a "firm unity of conviction," as William Penn observed, not by imposing a majority or narrow leadership's will (Endy 314). This means listening to perhaps even a single opposing voice, since that could well be the singular expression of wisdom or divine revelation. Neither majority nor minority may be right; rather a "sense of the meeting" arises only after all minds are "clear" thereby allowing unity. If serious difference remains, or a minority voice is held so deeply as to be unwilling to withdraw, the meeting will defer decision making, seeking later-unified clearness.

The novel's Sharer Gatherings are based upon similar Quaker-like efforts to discern right action in unity. Such Gatherings are central to the novel's plot movement as well as thematic development. We first experience a Sharer Gathering where the crucial struggle over Valon humanity is raised. Everything hinges on the potential for inward human confirmation of the off-worlders. Slonczewski has her protagonist Merwen express tentative doubt that the Gathering's proposed boycott of invading traders will elicit a necessary moral response against their harmful, addictive "gemstone" trading. Her concern is that proposed outward action will miss its sought after inward goal. She asks, "If Valens are our sisters, will our action reach into their hearts or will it glance away?" (86). Ironically, the boycott's outward action does succeed temporarily but it also precipitates Shora's military occupation by Valan troops. Speaking in a later crucial Gathering against those who now wish to respond with force to Valan brutality through a released virus, Merwen offers a solution more in keeping with traditional peaceful Shoran efforts: "'Consider this,' Merwen said at last. 'It may be that we can dispel the Valan plague by sharing force, as Yinevra suggests. I hesitate to guess what force the Valans will share in turn. It may be too late, afterward, to try to share mind healing instead'" (222). Out of the Gathering's Quaker-based centering silence, Merwen finds her empowerment to answer inwardly perceived truth: "In the stillness, Merwen reminded herself that as a wordweaver she had to weave not just her own words but those of all others into a truth that all could share" (976).

Her spoken opposition in the Gathering forestalls a violent, reductive response from "doorclosing" sisters. But the price Sharers must pay for sustaining their non-violent principles is high. Occupying soldiers are initially unsettled when hundreds of unarmed, naked Ocean women show up at their bases silently protesting the hostage taking of several Sharer sisters. General Realgar, their commander, is as much disconcerted by their physical nakedness, this "growing wall of purple flesh," as he is puzzled by their fearless, overtly fruitless tactics (244). Neither gas canisters, forced removal, nor finally extreme measures from a death-dealing guardbeam deter the non-violent protests. Additionally, Realgar is expressly embarrassed, and later violently angered, by his betrothed Lady Berenice, or Nisi as she is known among Sharers, who has gone native with her long-held sympathy for and identity with Shora culture. Lady Nisi goes about not only fully purple from the sea world's breathmicrobes, but as an adopted Sharer unclothed, a habit, or lack of habit, her male-possessive fiancée finds disapprovingly repugnant. Near the novel's end when Nisi has failed and been captured after a misguided attempt to blow up Realgar's headquarters, she is brought before the general for interrogation. His anger is compounded by her having been found Shora-naked: ". . .you sabotage my base, and my troops drag you in here shameless as a field whore" he rails (333). Losing control, he viciously strikes her, promising she will witness the execution of her co-conspirators. She protests she has acted alone and much against Shoran non-violence principles or their knowledge.

Realgar, who believes everything that has transpired on Shora makes sense only in terms of his own militaristic goals or patriarchal outlook, embodies the negative cultural clash between Shora/Valedon as well as the deeper underlying motif of understanding our humanity in the face of so much contrary evidence. The Valan youth, Spinel, appalled at the attrition and killing of thousands of witnessers, advises Usha: "You'll never make a Sharer of a Sardish soldier, not in a million years" (346). But Usha is far more hopeful of a good outcome: "It's not a matter of making, but of finding what is lost and buried" (346). Here we see a bedrock echo of Quaker belief in the Light, bearing witness to the Light already within others.

Spinel has himself partly metamorphosed (or found "convincement" in Quaker terms) as a "moon-creature," despite earlier fearing becoming "a monster," shaved hairless and turned purple-tinged by Shora's breathmicrobes. Nevertheless, his transformation from alien "male-freak" to an initiated self-namer and learnsharer among his adoptive sisters is fully realized in his growing love for Merwen's somewhat intractable daughter, Lystra, and their eventual acceptance of one another as lovesharers—despite the problematic evolved

Shoran sexual physiology. In Slonczewski's leading of Spinel into Sharer values there are various setbacks but also moments of insightful progress marking his gradual awakening. To encounter the other with respect for the other's shared humanity is to become a "selfnamer," one who recognitions the interwoven connections between all life. As Merwen instructs him, "A lesser creature sees a rival . . . and jumps in to fight it. A human sees herself and knows that the sea names her. But a selfnamer sees every human that ever was or will be, and every form of life there is. By naming herself, she becomes a 'protector' of Shora" (61).

Merwen herself, as a protector of Shora, is put to a final test of her own humanity as she confronts Realgar in his last attempts to break through to her resistance and in turn subjugate the entire planet. Earlier Realgar had declared with cold pronouncement: "You know that we will go on killing your sisters, until you obey or until you kill us." But Merwen asserts her defining human principal, observing Realgar is "dying already inside, from the sickness you call 'killing.'" Valens, she insists, must learn to share life not hasten death. For Sharers: "If we kill, we lose our will to choose, our shared protection of Shora, our ability to shape life. Our humanity would slip away, beyond even your own" (356).

That Slonczewski's central Sharer character is self-named Merwen the Impatient is itself is an interesting reflection of her Quaker-like struggle to maintain her faith in being able to reach the souls of Valans as well as keep before her moon sisters the power of continuing to witness Truth to the off-world humans. In a defining epistle at a time of internal discord and external strife, George Fox wrote to his co-religionists reiterating and encouraging their central doctrine:

> Go not forth to the aggravating part, to strive with it out of the power of God, lest you hurt yourselves, and run into the same nature, out of the life. For patience must get the victory and answer that of God in every one, must bring every one to it, and bring them from the contrary . . . . Therefore that which reacheth this witness of God within, and without in others, is the life and light; which will outlast all, which is over all and will overcome all. And therefore is the Seed of life live, which bruiseth the seed of death. (281)

If in Quaker terms there is not that which is of God in everyone, we are all terribly lost to our darkest impulses. Merwen has come to share distrust in her central vision of such redemptive goodness in all humankind. Such faith has been plunged into the visible darkness of the human soul, including her own.

She has had to glimpse the (dis)ease with which we all can diminish ourselves because we are able to demonize others made in the same image as ourselves, made ultimately in the image of God. Even Shorans, Merwen discovers, can share betrayal, of others and of self. Yet that very knowledge has paradoxically left her with the fuller realization that we still might resist submitting to our self-demons; we can, if sometimes only barely, avoid dragging ourselves into the dark hole of sub-human actions. Despite everything, in her darkest moment, Merwen has found healing confirmed in the Valedon male-freak Spinel. He has changed, answering to her of his humanness. Where once on his own world he had urged her to vengefully respond against "those who carry deathsticks," Spinel is now mind-healed. "That is why I still share hope with you," she now tells her tormentor General Realgar (380).

Realgar's seeming turnabout accord with her hope actually becomes a final entrapment. He has found a vulnerable weak link of her faith in human goodness, her investment in Spinel's change. Merwen is brought to Realgar's office not for further interrogation this time but to meet the boy. But Spinel is not only dressed in a soldier's uniform, he is armed with a deathstick. Here is fully-dressed Truth, so to speak: Spinel is one of them after all. Despite his denials he is dragged by guards from the room. Realgar then produces a holocube showing Spinel's deathstick murder of two witnessing Shora sisters. Overcome and with no experience of a doctored holo image, Merwen accepts this proof of Spinel sharing human betrayals. She plunges into whitetrance despair over an impending Sharer's self-induced death. Yet, before she sinks into whitetrance to seek this "Last Door" open to her, she offers these parting cryptic words to Realgar: "Though Spinel has shared my betrayal, you, Realgar, shall not" (382).

Faced with Shora's pacifist resilience in the face of his full military fury, Realgar's efforts to subdue the planet collapse as his troops' morale plummets and discipline turns with open sympathy toward what they realize is anything but a dangerous rebel force. As one sympathetic Valan officer declares to Usha: "A fool's war it's been, with no army to fight and no land to fight for" (373). The cost of course has been enormous in terms of their dead sisters and their shattered environment, and ultimately a soul transforming realization that the human impulse toward a killing hatred of one's declared enemies can destroy a trust in the good supposed to be at the center of the human soul. The novel remains ambiguously thin on this faith-held Quaker outcome. Can we somehow pull back from inflicted malevolence on our fellow human creatures? Is there after all that lifeshaping Light within, a Quaker-enacted witness to an inward Truth potentially answering our more egregious, destructive forces?

Yet, it would seem Slonczewski's contrastive utopian/dystopian struggle—symbolized by the Shora/Valan depiction of what is human—finds recognition of one's own and other's underlying demons, which can itself fan that small Light-flame within. Love's affirmation—the essential learnsharing of life itself—can heal our tarnished souls given even the slimmest of chances. So the novel's crucial denouement holds out.

At the novel's end, all save one of the principal characters are brought back through the door of darkness into Ocean's hope. Nisi the Deceiver has returned to Shora released from last minute possible execution by order of her former lovesharer. Realgar himself has been relieved of command and forced into a disgraced departure from the Shora moon world he could not subject to his own will and the Patriarch's rule. We last see him reflectively haunted by a mirror-glanced image into his own soul echoing the unanswered question Merwen had posed to him: "Whose eyes do you see in mine, and whose in [yours]" (399). Realgar remains linked to her witnessing the Light of his humanity, however strong the Valan's refusing denials.

Nisi, though returned, has "unspoken" herself over her violent betrayal of Sharer principals and as a penitent has withdrawn onto an isolated offshoot raft. Spinel, however, visits her to break through her self-imposed silence. The two reconcile in a symbolic acknowledgment of the ongoing struggle to change the assumptions of inevitable human violence and oppression. Yes, Valans will be banished from Shora, but these two can choose to stay in their adopted world of Sharer values. With pleading earnestness, Spinel declares he too will go unspoken and withdraw from the Gathering if Nisi doesn't break her silence and speak to him. But then Spinel, the self-named Impulsive, realizes he's over-stepped his own capacity. A less-than-thorough Quaker convert, he couldn't likely keep silent for a whole year: "I'd die for sure. Please, Lady Berenice." The noblewoman chides smilingly, "Spinel, you're still a commoner, after all." "Well," he replies shamefacedly, dismayed at how quickly he can revert to his old ways: "I can't change what I am overnight." Berenice reflectively agrees, acknowledging her own shortfall from Shora principal: "And yet, one can't stop changing either" (398).

The utopian task, despite reversions and setbacks, is still before them as a model of change and possibility—as for us as readers of the tale. Both characters have, in fact, made fundamental changes that are more than amethyst-skin deep. Spinel (the male-freak) and Nisi (the Deceiver) remain as neophytes in a world whose values they have tried to apprehend and embrace. Their mutual misapprehendings have been learnsharing, however, and will continue the iconic lifeshaping journey of Valon/Sharer reshaping.

Spinel has a last symbolic turnabout in the novel's final scene. Perhaps he should go back in duty to the world of his birth. There he might share learning and healing as a Spirit Caller. Through it all, Merwen had brought him to Shora to learn his own humanity as her "last bright hope for a oneness of Valan and Sharer" (291). Now in classic mono-myth terms, Spinel should return bringing salvic wisdom to his own people. Yet there's also the boy-meets-Edenic-girl myth too, foretelling the rebuilding of a fractured Shora. Stay and "Help raise our daughters . . ." (399), implores Lystra. Ok, she'll let him do what he must, but she'll not go to "that dry bone" alien world with him. At the last possible turning from boarding an outbound moonferry, Spinel chooses his greater investment in the future with Lystra as his lovesharer—score one for archetypal changed male-freak-meets-sensitive-feminist-girl-alien. With a message and a talismanic gift to his and Lady Nisi's old world, Spinel leaves the departing ship's captain. The gift is intended for delivery to Relgar's young daughter, but it is surely an expression to all Valens. The gift is small, a long promised "perfect worlshell polished by the sea" of Shora to Relgar's child. Also to be conveyed is a message to Realgar himself that Lady Berenice still loves him. With a last parting word of hope for his own Chrysoport home, "Just tell them, the door is still open" (402). Then Spinel dives from the water's edge searching ahead for the receding image of Lystra. He swims toward her with a message ringing in his own ears of "Come, lovesharer, come home" (406).

Robin Roberts, in her study of feminist utopias and the female alien, notes: "The novel details the reunion of the two worlds, the reunification of the species through Spinel (a Valan) and Lystra (his Sharer lover). . . . In a sense, Slonczewski holds out a possibility of communication between the feminine and the masculine, provided the latter relinquishes control over language and science" (144). That is, relinquishes those primary modes of patriarchy and hierarchical control that attempt to dominate rather than learn-share Shoran-Quaker values.

But it is something of a false dichotomy between returning/staying. As readers outside the text's referent imagery and thematic emphasis, we have witnessed the triumph of right over might, seen a violent subordinating culture unlearned—or at least unraveled—in the face of Quaker-echoing values and non-violent activism. We've witnessed prevailing feminist autonomy and embraced a non-hierarchical view of community. While still an alien-other world, we have been presented with a vision of enacted Sharer-Quaker possibilities. These become utopian values in our own reader-response hermeneutic. Like Spinel and Berenice, we answer the witness of Shora toward aspirations we already carry inwardly as being truly human. Likely not all lives, or invasions encountered, can be persuaded to non-violent, non-patriarchal, eco-feminist Sharer ways, but Slonczewski's Shora symbolically bears witness to such potential empowering: in Quaker terms recognition of *that which is of God in everyone.* Unrepentantly utopian, of course.

The paradox of utopia, contained in its etymological "no place," deconstructs perfect bliss for perfect blah as no place most of us can or would even want to inhabit, enforced or otherwise. But then dystopia as etymologically "bad" or "worst" place has little appeal as a zip code either. The utopia-dystopia tension, however, has much to offer as enstoried viewpoints of discontent with mostly avoidable human folly. Critic Gary Westfahl traces this science fiction paradox in an insightful essay. Both sides of utopia-dystopia remain inconsistent, incomplete, and unachievable, yet Westfahl concludes "…small victories in dispelling some ignorance are possible; [utopia-dystopia is] a world where ignorance can be vied with and sometimes conquered, though its final defeat is impossible" (239).

Aesthetically and narratively, *A Door Into Ocean* is a "vied with" attempt at appropriating a religious ideology to demonstrate enacted ways in which embraced Quaker values have and can achieve satisfying closure, settled consensus, and non-violent social action. All these decidedly non-mainstream Quaker characteristics as foregrounding and story undergirding provide a story social critique as well as modeling beyond the story confines: a utopian didacticism that allows an objectified assessment of believable human choice and consequence. Quakers after all are a peculiar people and stand in measured contrast to the usual mainstream struggles of social and political checks and balances. Quakers are not utopian in as much as they "speak Truth" to recognized human foible, as Slonczewski's story employs a spiritual/moral imperative that is not just idealized rhetoric but a practiced, applied lifestyle and life-witnessing ethic to many. Other human culture groups need not become Quakers (or Shorans) to answer the Light/Truth of those Quaker imperatives. So even if we are not thoroughly taken up by the authority and empowerment she offers, we still come away better understanding what has given form and experiential substance to her characters and the novel's resident themes.

Returning finally to Forrest J Ackerman's report card and earth's dismal "F" cosmic grade, Slonczewski through her symbolized final Shora/Valan union would seem to raise earth's report card to at least an encouraging "Incomplete" —holding out maybe for an eventual passing grade. Through Slonczewski's alien others, we have met our potentially mirrored and reshaped selves (at least on Shora) into our more humane Quaker-shaped selves.

✷ Works Cited ✷

Bauman, Richard. *Let Your Words Be Few: Symbolism of Speaking and Silence Among Seventeenth-Century Quakers.* Cambridge: Cambridge University Press, 1983. Print.

Endy, Melvin B. *William Penn and Early Quakerism.* Princeton University Press, 1973. Print.

Fox, George. *The Journal of George Fox.* Ed. John L. Nickalls. London: London Yearly Meeting of the Religious Society of Friends, 1975. Print.

Childress, James F. "Answering That of God in Every Man: An Interpretation of Fox's Ethics." *Quaker Religious Thought* 15. 3 (1974): 2-41. Print.

Heintz, Bonnie L., et. al., eds. *Tomorrow, And Tomorrow, And Tomorrow.* New York: Holt, Rinehart and Winston, Inc., 1974. 234. Print.

Levy, Michael M. "Feature Interview: Joan Slonczewski." *SFRA Review* 235/236 (Aug-Oct. 1998): 12-18. Print.

Roberts, Robin. *A New Species: Gender and Science in Science Fiction.* Urbana: University of Illinois Press, 1993. Print.

Schellenberg, James and David M. Switzer. "Interview with Joan Slonczewski." Online posting. Aug. 1998 <http://home.golden.net/~csp/interviews/slonczewski.htm>.

Slonczewski, Joan. *A Door Into Ocean.* New York: Avon Books, 1986. Print.

Westfahl, Gary. "Gadgetry, Government, Genetics, and God: The Forms of Science Fiction Utopia." *Transformations of Utopia: Changing View of the Perfect Society.* Ed. George Slusser, Paul Alkon, Roger Garllard, and Daniele Chatelain. New York: AMS Press, 1999. 229-41. Print.

Rex Stout

by Cathy Pitzer and Jean Mulhern

Rex Stout (1886 - 1975), of Friends lineage, was among the most celebrated mystery writers of the 20th century. In 1959, Stout won the Mystery Writers of America prestigious Grand Master Award. In 2000, along with Agatha Christie, Raymond Chandler, Dashiell Hammett, and Dorothy Sayers, he was nominated for the 2000 Bouchercon World Mystery Convention special award, Best Mystery Writer of the Century (won by Christie). Stout is best known for the creation of the corpulent detective Nero Wolfe and his wise-cracking legman, Archie Goodwin, who were featured in 47 novels, 40 novellas, and many short stories. The Nero Wolfe series had an unprecedented 40 year publishing run, selling over 100 million copies ("Rex Stout"). Today, many Stout titles are still in print and available as e-books, entertaining new generations of readers.

Rex Stout, Quaker

Can Rex Stout be considered a Quaker author? According to Stout's official biographer, John McAleer, Rex said that at age eleven he lost faith in God when his prayers went unanswered to keep his paternal grandfather nearby in Kansas rather than move to Chicago (72). Based on that youthful anecdote, Stout has been labeled an agnostic (McBride 90). Nevertheless, the evidence that Quaker values and influence and Stout's life were intertwined is strong. Notably, he avowed to live a life without violence, also at age eleven (McAleer 80). Gary Sandman, author of *Quaker Artists*, quotes on his website without source Stout saying at age 83, "I still think of myself as a Quaker, which may sound silly but isn't. Quaker background and influence must be an essential part of me..." (qtd. in Sandman "Rex Stout").

Rex Stout was born in 1886 to Quaker parents John William Stout, an Indiana newspaper editor, educator, and expert mathematician, and Lucetta Elizabeth Todhunter, from Wilmington, Ohio, and educated at Earlham College, a Quaker school. Both parents had been members of the Sand Creek monthly meeting in Bartholomew County, Indiana and transferred by certificate in 1885 to the Westfield meeting in Noblesville, Indiana (Sand Creek). Rex was born in Noblesville where his father was publishing a newspaper, but the family moved back to Kansas within the year and he grew up there, near his paternal Quaker grandparents and other relatives.

McAleer notes that as the father pursued careers as a newspaper publisher, school superintendent, and traveling encyclopedia salesman, the responsibility for rearing their many children was left to mother Lucetta, who was committed to Quaker faith and values, attending monthly meetings throughout her life whenever possible. McAleer concludes:

> ... it was her norms that prevailed. The influences brought to bear on Lucetta in the period of her own formation, and the way in which she responded to them, in keeping with her own distinctive temperament, had much to do, of course, with the precepts and outlook which she passed on to her children. (37)

Through McAleer we learn the details of Lucetta's "precepts and outlook." Lucetta was an insatiable reader who did not find fiction "frivolous" (40). She was a "sorceress" with flowers like her mother, Emily Todhunter (50), and not unlike Rex Stout and his Nero Wolfe. Growing up, she lived in an extended household that included as one of the family "Uncle Jack" Gantz, an African American employee of the Todhunters. Lucetta also participated in the care of several infirm relatives welcomed by the Todhunters (69). At age seven in 1893, Rex Stout enjoyed a pivotal summer vacation in Wilmington with his Todhunter grandparents and with Gantz as local guide (McAleer 64). Stout's maternal grandmother Emily Todhunter was a locally influential Quaker who actively promoted Wilmington College, social equality, and life-long education through reading. Her adult children were well-educated and she could count at least three nationally-known authors among her grandchildren, including Rex Todhunter Stout; Willis Todhunter Ballard, prolific writer of pulp mysteries and Westerns; and Rex's sister Ruth Stout, a memoirist who popularized organic gardening.

Lucetta was open-minded and eager to learn about other people and appreciate other ways of living. She rewarded individualism, independence and creativity in her children and encouraged adventure. One son, Robert, became a palm reader for a time and later a successful banker, daughter May was a doctor, and daughter Ruth worked at a Quaker orphanage in Russia (McAleer). Lucetta Todhunter Stout and her husband John were buried in a cemetery in New Jersey, their graves marked by plain headstones carrying their names followed by their death dates in Quaker date style (Find-a-Grave).

Rex joined the Navy rather than continue studies at the University at Kansas (McAleer 97-99). He acknowledged being a Quaker at age 30 when he registered for the World War I draft, a few years after he had served as a Navy-pay yeoman on President Theodore Roosevelt's yacht, the *Mayflower* (McAleer 100). Married at the time, Stout claimed religious exemption from the draft on grounds that he was a member of the "Society of Friends, Lawrence, Kansas" ("Rex T. Stout" 1917). Thus, for World War I he was a conscientious objector.

Quaker testimonies guide Friends in "ordering their lives," most prominently "peace, equality, integrity and simplicity" ("Quaker Testimonies"). Quakers espouse a peace testimony, which opposes military actions and war and promotes peaceful resolution of conflict. First stated in 1661, Quakers have interpreted this testimony in a variety of ways ("Friends Peace Testimony"). Rex Stout, acting on his family values and his own sense of peace, was put to the test with World War II. He set aside his lucrative creative writing and turned to supporting American defense activities by using his talents to create effective counter-propaganda initiatives including publications and broadcasting. His radio program effectively "busted" Nazi propaganda directed at the Allies (McAleer). His Associated Press obituary in 1975 highlighted Stout's actions as a Quaker:

> An early "one-worlder" and antifascist, Stout pursued his ideas to the lecture platform and the halls of government. Since 1941, when he was master of ceremonies of the "Speaking of Liberty" radio program, Stout had prompted [sic] the idea of world government. A Quaker who spoke out for an early entry into World War II and against a soft peace for Germany, Stout also was active on the "Voice of Freedom" and "Our Secret Weapon" radio programs during the war and headed the Writers War Board from 1941 to 1946. He also was president of the Society for the Prevention of World War III and chairman for more than 20 years of the Writers Board for World Government. ("Rex Stout, Creator of Nero Wolfe")

Quakers also have advocated strenuously for justice, most often grounded in the testimonies for equality and integrity. In that tradition, Stout was a life-long activist on behalf of authors' rights. In the 1920s, Stout was a close associate of Roger Nash Baldwin, a committed pacifist who had been imprisoned during WWI as a conscientious objector and founded the American Civil Liberties Union (ACLU). Baldwin recruited Stout to track censorship issues for the ACLU (McAleer 196-197). Stout served as president of the Authors League of America, later the Authors Guild, a professional organization for writers that, for more than a century, has provided advocacy on issues of free expression and copyright protection. Author John Jakes singled out Stout's service to his fellow authors through his League leadership: "Of his many activities, probably none was more important than his presidency of the Authors League Fund, which helps professional writers who happen to fall into dire financial distress" (viii). American author and journalist John Hersey said publicly, on the event of Stout's death in 1975:

> He was a noble man. His strength . . . lay in the deep-seated values he held to in human dealings—his decency, his generosity, his burning sense of justice—and yes, strange as it may sound, his humility. (Qtd. in McAleer 577)

Stout helped found the leftist Vanguard Press to assure a publication platform for authors less commercially mainstream. While serving as a Vanguard officer for five years, he oversaw the publication of 150 books, including seven titles by his friend Scott Nearing, a radical economist, pacifist, and advocate of simple living (McAleer 196-197).

In the Quaker tradition of laying out one's position on an issue for public consideration and the Stout family practice of spirited debate (McAleer), Stout publicly stated through two of his later novels his strong views on the primacy of "the morality of the civilized man" and refused to stand aside, based on his own core principles, even if it meant losing friends (Gifford). During the Vietnam era, Stout supported the war but condemned President Richard Nixon for Watergate and for subverting the Constitution. His last Wolfe novel, *A Family Affair (1975)*, has been called his Nixon novel, just as his *The Doorbell Rang* (1965) was his J. Edgar Hoover novel. These two novels overtly reflect Stout's negative views of those two contemporary controversial political figures. Best-selling thriller author and Stout fan Thomas Gifford observed, "Whatever Stout believed, he believed with passion."

Several aspects of Rex Stout's life align with the Quaker testimony of simplicity. He aspired to a literary career in France but put the support of his family first, seizing the more commercially viable route of writing popular mysteries while living with his parents, wife, and sister in New York City (McAleer). Later he built his own house "High Meadow" that pioneered the concept of residential simplicity in a plain form that settled well into a natural landscape that he tended daily. He was close to his family and to his extended circle of fellow authors and neighbors (McAleer).

Rex Stout was married twice. His first marriage to Fay Kennedy lasted 16 years but ended in divorce in 1932. Shortly after, he married Pola Stout, a textile designer of such renown that her obituary was published in *The New York Times* ("Pola Stout"). He had two daughters with Pola, and one of his grandchildren still lives in the family residence he constructed near Danbury, Connecticut (Wolfe Pack *Scrapbook*, 2013).

Rex Stout, Author

Rex Stout began his literary career with the publication of short stories and several serialized novels beginning in 1913, followed by his first published book *How Like a God* in 1929. By the time he died in 1975, Stout had more than 57 books in print, more than any other living American ("Rex Stout, Kansas"). Stout's first few books were fantasy and psychological novels, none of which were profitable. After losing in 1929 the fortune he had made by co-inventing (with his brother Robert) a school banking system, Stout focused on writing salable fiction to support his family. Stout explained, in a 1967 interview with Alfred Bester, how he came to write detective novels: "I realized that I was a good story-teller but would never make a good novelist, so I decided to write detective stories...of all kinds of stories the detective story is the most popular."

The first Nero Wolfe novel, *Fer-de-Lance*, was published in 1934 and was an immediate financial and critical success. Stout developed his characters in a period of American history considered to be the "Golden Age" of detective writing. However, both are oddly out of character with most detective writing of that day, which featured "hard-bitten," world-weary, pavement-pounding "P.I.s" ("Nero Wolfe and Archie Goodwin") such as Sam Spade, Philip Marlowe and Lew Archer (Yale-New Haven Teacher's Institute 2). In fact, Stout's younger first cousin, Willis Todhunter Ballard (1903 - 1980), began his commercially successful pulp-fiction writing career in the 1930s by creating a hard-boiled movie industry P.I., Bill Lennox, for *Black Mask Magazine* (Mertz). Ballard was educated in the Quaker institutions of Westtown and Wilmington College, across the street from his grandparents Amos and Emily Todhunter's house, Hackberry Hall.

Stout drew on his intimate knowledge of New York City to provide context for his Nero Wolfe detective series. Stout had lived with his parents and extended family on Morningside Avenue in 1910 and Central Park West in

1920 and in an apartment in the West Village in 1930 (US *Federal Census*). Stout's Nero Wolfe lived in a New York City brownstone on West Thirty-fifth Street, along with Archie, his assistant, Fritz Brenner, his chef, and Theodore Horstmann, who tended to Wolfe's orchids in his rooftop garden. Wolfe, in contrast to tough guy detectives, rarely left his townhouse and solved crimes by the power of deduction, in the tradition of similarly eccentric fictional detectives, such as Hercule Poirot and Sherlock Holmes. Wolfe's time, which was rigidly and inflexibly scheduled, was devoted to reading, eating gourmet meals, growing orchids, and solving crimes. Born in Montenegro, Wolfe was a naturalized U.S. citizen who was 56 years old throughout the series ("Nero Wolfe").

Archie Goodwin, who narrates the novels, was a tall, handsome ladies' man who was perpetually in his 30s. Archie handled most of Wolfe's contact with the world outside his brownstone. While Wolfe was a misogynist who had no romantic interest in women, Archie had a steady love interest, Lily Rowan, although he was involved with many other women throughout the series. Some suggest Stout's Wilmington, Ohio grandmother, Emily Todhunter, who was never far from her dictionary and beloved geraniums, provided the model for Wolfe (one of his novels begins with Wolfe tearing up the dictionary he always had on his desk). Stout himself, who has admitted to spending a lot of time investigating "the woman question" in his younger years, may be the model for Archie, who was said to be a native of Chillicothe, Ohio, not far from Wilmington ("Rex Stout is Alive…").

In his Nero Wolfe series, Stout sidestepped conflicts with his personal Quaker values of peace, integrity, and justice as he perfected the detective novel formula. His detective Nero focuses on the complex intellectual puzzle of uncovering and analyzing evidence to expose the guilty person. Wolfe would meet with a client in his brownstone, the client hired Wolfe to undertake an investigation – usually of a murder – and Archie served as his legman, bringing witnesses, information, and police to the brownstone. On occasion, Wolfe hired freelancers to help narrow down the suspects: Saul Panzer, Fred Durklin, Orrie Cather and Dol Bonner. Inspector Cramer of the NYPD and Lon Cohen, a newspaper reporter, completed the cast of characters. Eventually Wolfe identified the murderer and the case was closed when the murderer met an untimely death by accident or suicide. Stout did not pander to baser instincts with bloody shoot-outs or public executions, staying true to his own pacifist vow, even in his creative writing. Instead he created engaging plots in which society is not implicated in acts of violent retribution but readers still

QUAKERS AND THE DISCIPLINES

experience a final satisfaction in seeing the guilty criminal removed permanently (Beiderwell 15).

While Stout in many ways embodied Quaker values, Wolfe and Goodwin decidedly did not. Wolfe was obsessed with rather decadent interests, fine food and rare flowers, while Goodwin's interests, aside from detecting, focused on women. While both had a sense of fairness, neither was overtly interested in politics, social movements or world affairs, with the exception of *The Doorbell Rang* (1965), in which Wolfe took on the FBI. At least one critic believes Stout was "a deeply patriotic man who often subtly worked his concerns about American life into his mystery plots" ("Nero Wolfe and Archie Goodwin"), but Stout might disagree with this assessment. Stout's focus on personality, on "created characters" as he called them, rather than social problems, was intentional. In an interview Stout denigrated authors such as Phillip Roth and John Updike as writers who were interested in "sociology instead of people" (Shenker 263).

Which of the Nero Wolfe novels was the best? The largest number of readers would probably say *Some Buried Caesar* (1939). This novel is rather atypical in that Wolfe leaves his residence to exhibit his orchids and encounters the murder of not only a person, but also a bull named Caesar. This is also the book that introduces Lily Rowan, Goodwin's high-spirited main romantic interest. Other notable favorites include *The Doorbell Rang* (1965), which landed Stout a real life place on J. Edgar Hoover's "not to contact list" of persons considered to be hostile to the FBI, and the Zeck trilogy – Zeck was to Wolfe as Moriarty was to Sherlock Holmes - which culminates in Wolfe going undercover and losing 100 pounds in *In the Best Families* (1950). *A Family Affair* (1975), the last novel published before Stout's death, also ranks among his best.

One of the more interesting questions about Stout is his treatment of women in the Nero Wolfe novels. Wolfe is a misogynist, while Archie has a "girls in the typing pool" view of females. Few of the protagonists in Wolfe's books are women, although one of his earliest novels, *The Hand in the Glove* (1937), featured Theodolinda "Dol" Bonner as a rookie detective. Stout's stereotyped portrayal of women is somewhat surprising considering that his mother, sisters and aunts were all college-educated, professional women with the strong independent lives often associated with Quaker women. His wife Pola was an internationally accomplished designer who also created the supportive home environment in which he thrived as an author (McAleer). Perhaps Stout, surrounded in his personal life by strong women, enjoyed creating a masculine escape through the detective genre that avoided the emotional distractions of female relationships and focused on the entangled web of objective evidence. His detective novels were affairs of the mind, not of the heart.

Nero Wolfe novels maintained their popularity over the course of six decades, during which they spawned a comic strip, films, radio programs, several TV series, and even a Nero Wolfe cookbook. There is still an active Nero Wolfe discussion group on yahoo.com, and a Nero Wolfe fan club – The Wolfe Pack – where fans enjoy debating whether Wolfe and Goodwin actually existed and lived in a brownstone on the West Side of Manhattan. Interestingly, the Stout estate authorized journalist-turned-novelist Robert Goldsborough to continue the exploits of Nero and Archie. To date, Goldsborough has published nine titles, including *Murder in E Minor*, first written privately to please his mother, an avid Stout fan, who was devastated at the thought of not having new Nero/Archie mysteries. The Wolfe Pack, in support of the unusual arrangement, gave that first novel its Nero Award in 1986 (Goldsborough blog).

Why have Stout's novels maintained their popularity for such a long time? The mysteries are short, easy to follow, and well plotted. Furthermore, they are devoid of violence, gore and bad language, virtues that are mentioned by a surprising number of reader reviewers on sites such as Goodreads and by Robert Goldsborough, expert on Stout's writing style (Brown). Parents can share the books with older children without reservation. Stout's books provided enjoyable, easy to read diversions for decades of readers suffering through the Depression, World War II, the Cold War, Vietnam, Watergate and race riots.

Rex Stout, with deep American Quaker roots, evinced in his own life and in his writing the values of peace, integrity, justice, and simplicity associated with the Society of Friends as practiced by his Quaker parents and grandparents. The memory of his life well-lived is celebrated today by his grandchildren, who graciously receive his enthusiastic and loyal fans, and by the mystery writing and reading communities. Stout's most "Quakerly" achievement is the balance he achieved in his highly successful commercial fiction, especially his Nero Wolfe series. He adhered to an intellectually challenging and satisfying formula of detective fiction that is at the same time respectful of readers who abhor retributive violence.

✳ Works Cited ✳

"Authors and Creators: Rex Stout." *The Thrilling Detective Website*. Web. 10 July 2015. <http://www.thrillingdetective.com/trivia/rex_stout.html>

Beiderwell, Bruce. "State Power and Self-Destruction: Rex Stout and the Romance of Justice." *Journal of Popular Culture 27*.1 (1993): 13-22. Print.

Bester, Alfred. *Redemolished*. New York: ibooks, 2004. Web. 10 July 2015. <www.ibooksinc.com>

Brown, W. Dale. "Robert Goldsborough: The Whodunit." *Of Fiction and Faith: Twelve American Writers Talk about Their Vision and Work*. Grand Rapids, MI: Wm. B. Eerdmans, 1997. 161-181. Print.

"The Doorbell Rang." *Wikipedia*. Web. 10 July 2015.

"Friends Peace Testimony." Quaker Information Center, Earlham School of Religion, 2011. Web. 10 July 2015. <http://www.quakerinfo.org/quakerism/peace>

Gifford, Thomas. "Introduction." *Family Affair*. By Rex Stout. New York: Bantam/Viking, 1993. E-book.

Goldsborough, Robert. *Murder in E Minor*. NY: Bantam, 1986. Print.

---. Blog. 2014. Web. 10 July 2015. <http://www.robertgoldsborough.com/>

Goodreads. "Nero Wolfe Series." 2015. Web. 10 July 2015. <https://www.goodreads.com/series/51837-nero-wolfe>

Jakes, John. "Introduction." *Over My Dead Body*. By Rex Stout. NY: Random House, 2010. i - viii. Print.

McAleer, John. *Rex Stout, a Biography*. Boston: Little Brown, 1977. Print.

McBride, O. E. "The Literate Wolfe." *Stout Fellow: A Guide Through Nero Wolfe's World*. Lincoln, NE: iUniverse, 2003. 85-96. Print.

Mertz, Stephen. "W. T. Ballard: An Interview." *The Armchair Detective* (Winter 1979). Web. 10 July 2015. <http://www.blackmaskmagazine.com/ballard.html>

"Nero Wolfe and Archie Goodwin". *The Thrilling Detective* (2015). Web. 10 July 2015. <http://thrillingdetective.com/wolfe.html>

"The Psychology of Rex Stout, Nero Wolfe and Archie Goodwin." 2015. Web. 10 July 2015. <www.abelard.org/nero_wolfe.php>

"Quaker Testimonies." Earlham School of Religion. 2015. Web. 10 July 2015. <http://esr.earlham.edu/support/comprehensive-case/the-vine/the-quaker-testimonies>

"Rex Stout, Creator of Nero Wolfe." *Long Island Press* (Danbury, CT) 28 Oct. 1975. Web. 10 July 2015.

"Rex Stout is Alive and Arguing in Fine Fashion." *The Washington Post* 5 Oct. 1969. Web. 10 July 2015.

"Rex Stout, Kansas Author." *Map of Kansas Literature* (2015). Web. 10 July 2015. <www.washburn.edu/reference/mapping/stout>

"Rex T. Stout." (1917). New York, New York; Roll: 1766334; Draft Board: 130. U.S., World War I Draft Registration Cards, 1917-1918 [database on-line]. Provo, UT: Ancestry.com Operations Inc, 2005.

"Rex Stout." *Wikipedia*. Web. 10 July 2015.

Rollyson, Carl E. *Critical Survey of Mystery and Detective Fiction*. EBSCO Publishing: eBook collection, 2008. E-book.

Sand Creek Monthly Meeting Minutes. (1885). *U.S., Quaker Meeting Records, 1681-1935* [database on-line]. Provo, UT: Ancestry.com Operations, Inc., 2014.

Sandman, Gary. "Rex Stout." *Quaker Artists*. 2011. Web. 10 July 2015. <http://www.quaker.org/fqa/sandman.html>

---. *Quaker Artists*. 2nd ed.Columbia, SC: Kishwaukee Press, 2015. Print.

Shenker, Israel *Words and Their Masters*. New York: Doubleday, 1974. Print.

Stout, Rex. *The Doorbell Rang*. NY: Viking, 1965. Print.

---. *A Family Affair*. NY: Viking, 1975. Print.

---. *Fer-de-Lance*. NY: Farrar & Rinehart, 1934. Print.

---. *The Hand in the Glove*. NY: Farrar & Rinehart, 1937. Print.

---. *How Like a God*. NY: Vanguard Press, 1929. Print.

---. *In the Best Families*. NY: Viking, 1950. Print.

---. *Some Buried Caesar*. NY: Farrar & Rinehart, 1939. Print.

United States *Federal Census* (1910, 1920, 1930). [database on-line]. Provo, UT: Ancestry.com

The Wolfe Pack. 2015. Web. 10 July 2015. <www.nerowolfe.org/htm/stout>

The Wolfe Pack Scrapbook (2013). "The Wolfe Pack Visits High Meadow." Web. 10 July 2015. <http://www.nerowolfe.org/htm/scrapbook/2013_High_Meadow/index.htm>

"Works of Robert Goldsborough." *The Wolfe Pack* (2015). Web. 10 July 2015. <http://www.nerowolfe.org/htm/corpus/Goldsborough>

Yale-New Haven Teacher's Institute. *Plot, Character and Setting: A Study of Mystery and Detective fiction*. 2015. Web. 10 July 2015. <www.yale.edu/ynhti/curriculum/units/1989.4/89.04.09.x.html>

✳ 5 The Practice of Writing: A Quaker Poet's Perspective ✳

Beyond the Inward Light:
The Quaker Poet in Community

by William Jolliff

It's a privilege to be granted a chance to address a gathering like this: a room full of people whose Quaker way of life and thought are so very central to their work that they spend time and resources to get together and talk about it. We've been blessed with a common gift, and it isn't a small one.

That said, I suspect I'm not the only one here who sometimes wonders how, or even if, what I do matters. Yet even among you, my group of fellow self-doubters, I must lobby for my own elevated position: as a poet and a teacher of poetry writing, I have the privilege of practicing the discipline *most* often used to exemplify the frivolous.

That I don't accept the characterization of poetry as *frivolous* should go without saying, though sometimes in discussions I can do little more than bite my lip and try to recall the words of William Carlos Williams:

> It is difficult
> to get the news from poems
> 　yet men die miserably every day
> 　　for lack
> of what is found there.

More than once, I've counseled with students or prospective students who feel a pull toward something in my field, scholarly or artistic, but who simultaneously suspect that they might be better paid—or of better service— feeding the hungry, healing the sick, creating a new Smartphone application,

111

running for public office, or sailing off to the hinterlands to carry the Gospel. All good things, of course. And I readily admit that for many or nearly all students, those avenues of service might be better.

If, however, you'll grant me for the next fifty minutes the possibility that poetry matters, what I want to address today is a more focused question: What is the role of a *Quaker* poet? Historically, Quakers have never been champions of the frivolous, but I am asking that question anyway. And, because I think our lives are inevitably lived out among others, What is the role of the Quaker poet in community? I'll even parse that question further: How does a Quaker poet do good and Friendly service in the place where he or she is situated—using the word *situated* in both the inner and outer sense, the spiritual and physical?

Some of you are poets; more of you are not. For those of you who are not poets, this talk may well be tedious. But it's possible that the trajectory I take will find a parallel in your own field. I'll trust that you can make the analogical leap without too much of my help, since in all likelihood I couldn't give it, anyway.

If I make any more disclaimers, you'll assume this is a meeting of worship for business and slip off to the meeting house kitchen, so I'd best get on with the work at hand:

What is the role of the Quaker poet in community?

I am enough of a traditional, dyed-in-the-wool academic to begin my exploration by leaning hard toward the problem, putting my shoulder firmly to the wheel, and focusing my best line of sight squarely backwards.

I'll begin, Friends, with Whittier.

I doubt that it ever occurred to the *poet* John Greenleaf Whittier that his work didn't matter—any more than it did to the *political lobbyist* Whittier or the *journeyman journalist* Whittier. For the simple reason that it so clearly did matter.

Whittier was, after all, the great abolitionist poet. When he felt the call of God—as delivered by God's proxy, William Lloyd Garrison—to leave behind his life as an opportunistic journalist and give himself over to the cause of the slave, it did not occur to him to leave behind the craft he dreamed might make him an American version of Robert Burns. By God's/Garrison's decree, Whittier carried his poetry with him into the greater community, the public argument, as his most important persuasive tool; and not only did it go with him but, as I have argued elsewhere, the gift, and the drive to exercise that gift, was intensified (Jolliff 17-20).

It's difficult for us to think of using poetry as a way of influencing popular thought. Indeed, the reasons for Whittier's maintaining his poetic craft become clear only if we understand his calling in its historical, cultural context.

In his day, there was nothing frivolous about the influence of poetry. To begin, poetry was a popular art form. Regular people read regular poetry. Regular everyday newspapers had poetry pages. And when regular people read regular poetry in the regular columns of their regular newspapers, they expected it to be about something that would pertain to them: tales of lost love and sentimental celebrations of hearth and home were versified, of course, but poetry also had a place as informed opinion on the most pressing issues of the times.

Now it was as natural for a nineteenth-century citizen to read the poetry page of the local paper as it is for you and me to get in the car and click on the radio.

And when we turn on the radio, we very likely do not struggle, at least very much, to discern what the newscaster means or what the songs we listen to mean. The newscaster's script is written to be readily understood by anyone, and the songwriter's lyrics likewise. Beyond a basic education, it was not necessary in Whittier's day to have specialized training to read a poem any more than it demands of us specialized training to grasp the content and intention of our own media personalities, folks like Rush Limbaugh or Brian Williams or Taylor Swift.

So if 160 years ago you had picked up *The National Era* or *The Liberator* or many other papers and turned to a Whittier poem, you would have understood it perfectly well. That's what his poetry was written for: to be understood. It was art, yes, but art for popular consumption—and more. And it is indeed likely that you would have seen a Whittier poem. Because even though he might have been publishing his poems in various minor local and regional papers, that was not the range of a poem's life. Here's why.

Nineteenth-century newspapers had *exchange* desks. Newspaper editors purchased or exchanged subscriptions with other editors, and they used the other papers' published material freely. That was not plagiarism; it was accepted practice. So a Whittier poem might appear in a little paper in Hartford or Amesbury, then find itself exchanged with a paper in Boston, then exchanged with a paper in New York, then exchanged with papers in Washington, DC, or Atlanta or Cincinnati, so that instead of having a few hundred readers or a few thousand, that poem might potentially have a few hundred thousand. Therefore, if some activist had a concern—the horrific plight of the slave, for example—to take to the masses, as hard as it may be to believe today, poetry might well have been a perfectly functional, expedient avenue to reach the broadest community.

Now this is something you must keep clear: in seeking a contemporary cultural comparison with Whittier, you shouldn't think in terms of Whittier as parallel to Li Young Lee or Charles Wright or even Ted Kooser; yes, they are great poets of our day, but they are, from any pop cultural standpoint, utterly obscure. That was not Whittier. Think *Springsteen*. Think *Bono*. Think—and why not?—*Miley Cyrus*.

My point is that he had a huge potential audience for his abolitionist poetry. A huge audience. A great potential for Friendly ministry through poetry. The culture at large read Whittier's poems just as people now listen to sad songs and love songs and talk radio, just as they click open the *Times* and read the op-ed page!

Poetry today is in a different position. The function once held by poetry in popular culture is now filled by other art forms, other media. The gratifications poetry has always offered persist, but in very different forms. The long rhythmic narratives that Whittier and his kin saw as their real contribution long ago gave way first to the novel, then to films, and now to whatever new binge-ready series Netflix offers. The lyrical love poems of Whittier and his kin have been displaced by popular song. The political commentary of Whittier and his kin now falls within the pale of Bill O'Reilly or Amy Goodman or whatever talking head the pharmaceutical giants and their networks deem worthy—worthy to tell the national tale and sell their Cialis.

Poetry and Media

Since the avenue of poetry as a broadly circulating popular medium is gone, today's Quaker poets must rethink, radically rethink, the role of their work in their communities. The popular community does not exist for the twenty-first-century Whittier. So as poets, as Quaker poets, as champions of the frivolous in plain coats, where do we minister? How do we minister? What communities might we serve? We need to reconsider many questions, the most obvious being scale.

Thankfully, poetry does maintain one other little niche or ten in our culture. I'll offer you three, with no intention of being comprehensive.

Niche #1: Let's start with self-discovery, the examined life. Such helping folks as school teachers, spiritual directors, and the occasional counseling psychologist may still direct their students or clients to write out their feelings in poetry. Contemporary free verse, with its apparent lack of hard-wrought craft, especially lends itself to such outpourings, and these are good. But they aren't, for the most part, anything anyone else would want to read. They perform a helpful and necessary function for the growth of the individual, and maybe the act of expression itself can be a kind of witness; but generally these "poems" find that their best or only audience is an audience of one, maybe, maybe two. How might a Quaker minister in such community settings?

Very well, I believe. I'd even say it's right up our Friendly alley. As teachers who help students find a voice for dreams and fears, as spiritual directors who help directees look closely at their own souls, as counselors who help clients make sense of their past, their present, and their full human potential, a Quaker way of walking through the world can readily find opportunity for ministry. The Friendly potential for doing good in such contexts—and maybe that's what I mean by the Quaker's place in community—is clear.

I assure you that it is not an easy, natural thing for most people to let their deepest feelings, their darkest memories, fall unmediated into words; and the Quaker teacher, spiritual director, or counselor who is skilled in the powers of poetic discovery can be a Friendly paraclete who helps that happen. The poetic *craft* in such contexts comes in as we learn for ourselves and teach others the invention skills, the exploratory methods, the powers of figurative comparison, the surprising recognitions in narrative form, even the places of non-judgmental expression—those techniques that make the way open for everyday miracles. So that's one potential place for ministry.

Niche #2: Now let's jump to the opposite end of the spectrum: the enduring place of poetry in the world of what I will crudely call high art. When poetry ceased to be a popular form, when it became the stuff of artistic specialists, its forms changed utterly. What may seem to the uninitiated like craftless expression is, in fact, often following complex sets of principles, a challenging prosody that would never have been conceived by Whittier or Longfellow or, dare I say it, Shakespeare. In the context of high art, there has never been a time when poets were more obsessed with the challenges of form. The result is that high art poetry is now the stuff of universities, of devotees with developed tastes for specialized art, and of course other poets. High art indeed! Much of it is intensely difficult, even off-puttingly so.

Poetry has gone the way of the other high arts, but it's gone further and it's traveling without much of a trust fund.

Let me add, however, one more complicating factor: with the displacement of traditional Anglo-American prosody and poetic forms by free verse, the most easily accessible and immediately gratifying aspects of poetic craft have fallen away. What high art contemporary poetry has gained in sophistication it has lost in accessibility. Just as it's easier for most people to find gratification in the works of Thomas Hart Benton than in those of Jackson Pollock, it's easier to discern and find pleasure in the craft of William Shakespeare than William Stafford, easier to find pleasure in the work of John Donne than of John Ashbery. Again, that isn't bad, and it isn't good. It simply is.

How does the Quaker poet find a way to contribute to, to minister in, that high art community?

The answer here is rather straightforward: If serious poetry is your gift or passion, you simply do your art and earn your place in that community. The Quaker poet can and should have a role in that world, practicing her craft with excellence and rigor just as a Quaker painter or sculptor or novelist or composer practices her craft with rigorous expertise. And ideally, the foundational noetic constructs of that poet or painter are informed by Quaker ways of being in the world. Even with accomplishment and professional success, one's audience is inevitably small, the community served will be small; but that doesn't mean that the art doesn't have weight, that it doesn't have cultural significance.

Niche #3: Let me suggest a third kind of community that can be served by the Quaker poet: what I'll call the remnant of a popular audience. When poetry is published by *Sojourners* or *Christian Century* or our own *Friends Journal*—or on the back of your monthly meeting's worship folder—the editors are, knowingly or unknowingly, banking on the fact that some poetry may still be enjoyed, may still be edifying for an audience that is not exactly the high art audience of the literary arts journal. They are banking on the fact that just as some of us go *occasionally* to a gallery or symphony, some of us *occasionally* read poetry. The readers in the remnant may be few, the readers who benefit by the ministry of the poem may be fewer yet, but that certainly doesn't mean the ministry shouldn't be performed in, offered to, such a community.

What the poet must keep in mind for successful ministry in this remnant community, however, is that the readers must be able to access and be gratified by, at least after a reading or two or three, what the poem offers. That means, it seems to me, that the poem must be something more craft-rich than therapy; and at the same time, it must be more accessible than what one might offer in a more rigorously craft-intensive form of high art.

The Role of the Poet

Trying to discover my own potential role as a poet in each of these communities, if indeed I am to have one, as a Quaker and as a poet who works in a not-very-accessible contemporary style, has led me to do some good amount of soul-searching around the question of what I have to offer of myself, what I have to offer the artistic community, and what I have to offer a somewhat broader, if rather small audience; and most of all, to consider how my Quaker way of walking through the world can inform my own thought and work.

I have to ask (1) which elements of my contemporary poetic craft might aid the soul-searcher who learns personal expression as a way of growth, (2) which elements of my craft might be developed by the best artistic craft of the day as practiced by those in the high art community, and (3) which elements of my craft might remain sufficiently accessible to allow a worthy pay-off for the remnant, what we might risk calling a general readership. And how may I practice this in a contemporary mode, the formal aspects of which are tremendously and simultaneously difficult and subtle?

As I have struggled with these tasks, with these three communities, I've found, ironically maybe, that the various ultimata they present may all be compressed into that very same question every free-verse poet has fielded from some well meaning student or reader or listener:

What makes that stuff you do poetry?

"I get 'Gunga Din,'" the question goes, "now buddy, that's poetry. But what's with so much depending on that red wheel barrow glazed with rain beside the white chickens?"

And in fact, that's a question I've been asking myself for nearly fifty years.

Having tired of asking it and being asked, I have decided to answer it, for good or ill. As it happens, I think my answers come from a place where my Quakerism and my craft converge. Those of you who are poets may well here see me as having let my despair turn into prescriptive dogmatism. But those of you who are not poets may be about to encounter the first understandable answer you've ever heard—take that as one of the blessings of reductionism.

I'm going to spend my remaining minutes, then, offering the Poetry Gospel according to St. William: my answer to the question, What makes a free verse poem a poem?

I will preface my answer by saying that poetry is *spiritual.* There, I've said it. In spite of the fact that spiritual seeking has been my most important concern for half a century, I learned early on as an academic never to use the word *spiritual.* If you work in a university environment, you soon learn that even among religious academics, questions of spirituality are often brushed courteously or discourteously aside, not because they are unimportant but because such questions don't lend themselves to the ways of knowing most current in academe.

These days, however, I'm trying to let myself be a little more open, a little more crass, a little more ruthless, a little more free with spiritual language. And here's why: I need it. I've come to the conclusion that poetry, and much of literature, maybe much of what we study in all the arts and sciences, can't really be discussed intelligently and rigorously if one whole aspect of what it means to be human is bracketed off, relegated to other, lesser arenas, ghetto-ized to religious institutions, coffee shops, or the silence of one's own room.

Even as you hear this, I suspect that some of you may be getting uncomfortable with the direction my discussion is going: if so, your teachers have trained you well!

So let me assure you that this isn't where I try to sign you up for a crusade or a *jihad*, ask you to disrobe, or even to hold your pen in a magical way and hum "OOOOMMMM" (though you may do all three if you wish). When I use the word *spiritual* in the moments to come, what I'm referring to, more or less, are those elements of our shared human experience that don't lend themselves easily to empirical, objective analysis; but, rather, offer themselves to a kind of shared subjective analysis. My feeling of love or transcendence is not yours, and it doesn't lend itself to some kinds of examination. That's true. But the fact that you, too, might have similar psychological experiences or even physical manifestations is certainly reason enough for us to talk about them—to compare notes, if nothing more. (Do you recall the first time you quaked before the Lord?)

There are things that we cannot analyze empirically, necessarily, but which have been important, for good reasons, to humans of many cultures and many ages and which, right now, you share, to one degree or another, with everyone you know and don't know. And I'd like to suggest that those things are the very stuff of much of the best poetry. Even when it doesn't seem like it.

Now on to the question: "What makes *that* thing a poem?"

If free verse apparently, *apparently*, fulfills no readily defined standard of craft, if it has no rhyme, and if it has no regular meter, how do I know when I've written a poem? Exactly what does make that page of language become a poem?

Delight. To begin, a poem must call special attention to itself *as language*, and the attention paid must reward the reader with delight. If meaning is all that I gather from having read a particular chunk of language, it's not a poem. (Some would even argue that poetry should be relatively free of meaning. I don't.)

Now that sounds a little dogmatic, and it is. But it is saved from terrible narrowness by this wondrous fact: there are infinite ways for language to give delight, ways that are very traditional (like rhyme, meter, and figures of speech), contemporary (like the position of the words on the page, like line breaks that play against syntax and force multiple simultaneous meanings, like the subtle musicality of vowels, etc.), and radically innovative (like those I haven't thought of yet, but that maybe you will). If a chunk of language says, "Look at me, I'm not your run-of-the-mill soup bowl of words—I give you delight just by my own, uh, something-or-other, that little bit of bliss you felt when reading me," then that chunk of language has met *the most essential* demand of poetry. If it does not offer delight, it is not a poem.

But a poem must be more than craft that leads to delight. And here I'll become very prescriptive: In addition to the delight factor, a poem must allow the reader to experience one of these three qualities: identification, transcendence, and epiphany. By the way, I suspect these qualities often overlap and ultimately get a little hazy. Don't worry about that. I'm being dogmatic, so you don't have to.

Identification. This quality is, I think, the one that happens most frequently in a good contemporary poem. By identification, I mean that the poem must make the reader feel something in common (identification) with the experience of the poem's implied speaker. That's simple Aristotle. When I first conceptualized this idea in relation to poetry, I referred to it in my own notes as the *ain't-that-just-the-way-it-is* factor, and I think I still may prefer my term to Aristotle's. Consider your favorite story or your favorite song. I suspect it's a favorite because it communicates something true and meaningful about your own experience of life as lived. Maybe you identify with the anger, or the joy, or the lousy tricks experience plays on a person.

It's the same with a poem, but it might obtain on a different scale. Sometimes the experience of identification in a poem might simply be, "Yes, I feel the same way when the sky looks like that in the morning." Or "Yes, I feel the same way when I run across my daddy's high school photographs." Or "Yes, I feel that same isolated, lost-in-the-world way when my cell phone dies in the airport." The degree of emotion, the importance of the predicament, the weightiness of the topic—those things don't necessarily matter. What matters is the "I feel the same way. . . ." part. That means that the poem has hit upon something true about the broader human condition, often in a very personal way. That's identification. And because the feeling takes us outside ourselves and situates us deeper in a common humanity, it's a spiritual thing.

What better for a Quaker poet to do than lead one of her fellow humans to that place of shared humanity?

So if after you've read a chunk of language you can honestly say, "Ain't that just the way it is"—and if the language itself gives you a little delight—then that poem has justified itself as a poem.

Transcendence. Because it's been used in so many contradictory ways, *transcendence* can be a confusing term. Don't let it be. In its most basic sense, to transcend simply means this: to cross a boundary. Sometimes a poem will be rambling on about something perfectly mundane—cooking squash, waiting for traffic light to change, fishing without catching any fish, etc. But by the time you get to the end of the poem, often right at the end of the poem, or maybe on the third reading, you realize that there is an abundance of significance—and yes, I'll use the term—a *spiritual* significance, in that mundane event.

A boundary has been crossed: you thought you were just reading a delightful mix of language apparently about waiting on a traffic light, but somewhere you began to realize that you, along with the speaker, were struggling against the very nature of the human relationship with the disheveled reality of time . . . or, well, something like that. Generally you *feel* the transcendence first, before you verbalize it in your mind. And in fact, nothing says that as a reader you ever have to verbalize it *at all*—or even fully make sense of it. Often you won't. You only know that for some reason you really like the poem, you want to read it again, and you want to read the next one in that literary journal or magazine or book. You know that *something is there*, that the poem has significance that crosses the boundary from the mundane matters of the flesh to the extraordinary matters of the spirit. You've been reading about particulars, but experiencing universals—something more deeply, more meaningfully human, than waiting to turn off the stove or try another bait or press the accelerator pedal.

What better gift might a Quaker poet give than to help one's fellow humans occasionally cross that line?

Epiphany. *Epiphany* is a term I'm borrowing from Christian religious tradition and, to a lesser degree, modernist literary criticism. In literary criticism, an "epiphany" is a moment of sudden understanding. But in the Christian tradition, an epiphany is the appearance of God (in one form or another). Maybe it's the recognition of divine immanence. I think that some poems are accounts of epiphanies, and that if the poem does its job well, we as readers not only understand the account presented but have just a taste, an insinuation, of the epiphany itself. One needn't hold particular—or, indeed, any—religious views to appreciate the poem as a piece of art that relates an experience the speaker perceives as an appearance of God. But I suspect that poems with the quality of epiphany are most easily enjoyed by people who themselves have some belief in the possibility of divine encounter, of the possibility of recognizing the immanence of the holy.

The immanence of the holy.

It would seem right away that such poems would be extraordinarily rare. And if the only poems we could classify as *epiphany* were those relating the first-person experiences of wrestling with angels or being handed some big stone tablets scratched with commandments, such would be the case. But that's not quite what I'm getting at.

Think of Ralph Waldo Emerson suddenly feeling at one with the universe while stepping in a mud puddle on Harvard Square, of Walt Whitman seeing the mysteries of the universe displayed in a spear of summer grass, or of Mary Oliver hearing the perfect prayer in a flock of terns. These things fall under my category of epiphany—a deep-felt experience of the Divine in the commonplace.

Any serious artist, Quaker or otherwise, must pursue her craft with a continual awareness of the demands of contemporary practices and the expectations of contemporary audiences. And to be certain, reading and writing free verse poetry is quite a different experience from reading and writing traditional, Whittier-type poetry. But possibly these reflections have opened you to the possibility that maybe, just maybe, it's not quite as different as you may have thought. Many of the characteristics of free verse poetry are more subtle versions of the characteristics of traditional poetry, and others are not subtle at all; they may even be more intense. For people who strive to read well, both kinds of poetry can provide a satisfying, even a spiritual, reading experience. And for people most open to the spiritual aspects of their lives, poetry may well become one of the important ways they travel through—and make sense of—their days on this earth.

I hope this discussion has been an encouraging one. Quaker poets have good work to do; and it's work which lends itself, through its processes and by its products, to the living expression of Friendly principles. That writing poetry is hard work is no surprise. That it is good work, even essential work, is something of which we doubters sometimes need to be reminded.

In summary then, these are the ways I believe that the Quaker who ministers through poetry can serve her communities:

(1) She can, if her gifts allow, use the powers of poetry to teach people new and expedient ways of wisdom-nurturing self-exploration and healthful self-expression;

(2) She can, if her gifts allow, take her place in the "high art" world of serious poetry and do so with a Quaker sensibility that bears weight in the broader culture; and

(3) She can, if her gifts allow, speak to a broader audience with good, gratifying, accessible poems.

Through creative work that offers delight and that faithfully offers the experience of identification, transcendence, or epiphany, the Quaker can minister to a community or communities. We will never be John Greenleaf Whittier or Rush Limbaugh or Taylor Swift, but there's nothing frivolous about our work. For some of us, it's even a calling.

✳ Works Cited ✳

Jolliff, William, ed. and intro. *The Poetry of John Greenleaf Whittier: A Readers' Edition*. By John Greenleaf Whittier. Richmond, IN: Friends United Press, 2000.

Williams, William Carlos. "Asphodel, That Greeny Flower." *The Norton Anthology of Modern and Contemporary Poetry*. Eds. Jahan Ramazani, Richard Ellmann, Robert O'Clair. New York and London: W.W. Norton, 2003. 311-317. Print.

✳ 6 The Practice of Teaching: Towards a Quaker Literary Pedagogy ✳

User-Friendly Theatre:
The Implications of Quaker Faith and Practice On Presentational Dramatic Performance

Darlene R. Graves

Unless the theatre can ennoble you, make you a better person, you should flee from it.

— Constantin Stanislavski

This paper looks at some of the recent Quaker contributions to the theatre as a striking contrast to early Quaker rejections of the theatre. The Quaker experience with the arts, and theatre specifically, can be viewed as "a turning of seasons" from a three-century long winter of brittle schism to a twentieth-century spring of budding promise, bearing significant artistic fruit.

The elements that set the schism—and what prompted the promise—will be the focus of the first half of this essay. After outlining the Quaker antagonism toward theatre and then presenting the occurrences that led to the start of healing the rift between Friends and the arts, I will explore some attributes of Quaker faith and practice that actually inspire and support a style of creative and improvisational drama. Finally, I will propose that these same practices may help to guide traditional theatre processes toward developing a more satisfying artistic process and product, depending on the individual directorial proclivities.

123

Ironically, the very doctrines and disciplines of the Society of Friends, which prompted their suspicion and rejection of what was considered "worldly" Art—particularly theatre art—in the seventeenth, eighteenth and nineteenth centuries, may have prompted them to consider eventually embracing that prodigal in the twentieth century. Although some Quakers are still not ready to bestow the blessing ring and kinship cloak carte blanche to all of theatre, others have participated more willingly in a reunion festival welcoming home the arts.

In her article *Art and Integration*, Katherine Lesses noted that at the beginnings of the Quaker movement in the seventeenth century there were many reasons for a suspicious attitude towards art, since usually

> ... works of art were financed by established political and religious institutions and used to legitimize them. In this connection, the arts took on a tinge of immorality. The appreciation of artistic products on purely aesthetic grounds, unrelated to any serious content, led to the belief that art was frivolous, and the practice of the arts, other than for specific religious purposes such as journal writing, occupied time and energy that should be devoted to other causes. (128)

Quakers were serious and forthright, particularly in their early rejection of theatre. Robert Barclay roundly condemned the theatre in his influential *Apology for the True Christian Divinity*, first published in English in 1678. In Proposition fifteen, he asserted:

> ... these games, sports, plays, dancing, comedys, etc. ... were invented to pass away the precious time, and divert the mind from the witness of God in the heart. . . they do naturally tend to draw men from God's fear, to make them forget heaven, death, and judgment, to foster lust, vanity, and wantonness. (343)

That this general antagonistic attitude toward the theatre continued among the Society of Friends for at least two more centuries is evident in the comment made by Henry Ward Beecher, as published in an 1857 edition of *The Friend:*

> If you would pervert the taste—go to the theatre. If you would imbibe false views—go to the theatre. If you would efface as speedily as possible all qualms of conscience—go to the theatre. If you would put yourself irreconcilably against the spirit of virtue and religion—go to the theatre. If you would be infected with each particular vice in the category of depravity—go to the theatre. Let parents who wish to make their children weary of home's domestic enjoyments take them

to the theatre. If it be disirable [sic] for the young to loathe industry and didactic reading, and burn for fierce excitements and seek them by stealth through pilfering, if need be—then send them to the theatre. (Qtd. in Eddington 14)

Even in the early blush of the twentieth century, it was evident that Quakers still held a certain contempt for the theatre and its conceded power to draw pure minds toward vice and vanity. This attitude is reflected in the following quotation found in the 1908 *Principles of Quakerism* drawn up by the Friends in Pennsylvania, New Jersey and Delaware:

> Friends believe that Christians should not go to see theatrical performances, first, because acting is essentially demoralizing to the actors. The fact that some men and women of the stage accept and follow the ordinary laws of morality, in no way weakens this objection. The demoralizing effect of the whole atmosphere and surroundings of stage life is recognized by many of those engaged in it. Secondly, Friends are opposed to theatre-going because of its effect on those who go. Everybody condemns bad plays, but who shall say where the line shall be drawn? Most of the plays patronized by the better class of people contain passages which are objectionable from the point of view of strict morality. Add to this the unwholesome artificial mental excitement produced by watching plays, and the questionable associations into which play-going leads, and it becomes sufficiently evident that the practice is adverse to spiritual growth. (194-195)

We could wonder what kind of impact this statement would have now if read in our meetings when considering the current content and influence of contemporary theatre within the contexts of television and film as it has re-entered daily conversations. Indeed, the contemporary state of media affairs is causing considerable concern. Historically, however, early Friends were eventually open to some social adjustments to the arts in general. In the first part of the twentieth century, Friends began to reflect on other changes in the surrounding British and American cultures which led, subsequently, to a relaxation of Quaker rejection of music as an initial step. In addition, Quakers eventually developed and supported their own liberal arts and Bible colleges in America. It appears the institutions of higher learning thus provided centers for intellectual and cultural debate which ultimately relaxed the fierce Quaker opposition to the arts as a whole and encouraged a glance in that direction with an altered eye.

A broader intellectual dialogue among The Society of Friends, which eventually sparked a focused concern on the potential redemption of the arts, began with a series of "Swarthmore Lectures" delivered in England. Kenneth C. Barnes, a respected Quaker scientist and artist, lectured in 1960 on *The Creative Imagination* and prodded the Society's concern about the arts with the notion that "if we have faith in the unity of God and Truth, we should have the courage to follow where Truth leads" (27). Almost two decades later, in 1978, J. Ormerod Greenwood presented a Swarthmore Lecture published as *Signs of Life*, in which he also argued that denying the range of experience found in the arts involved a denial of part of oneself. Moving forward, Laurence Lerner's 1984 Swarthmore Lecture, *The Two Cinnas*, postulated that the artist is a kind of prophet. Thus, a wide swath of acceptance was made in a rather short span of time, considering the previous sluggish history of rejection.

During this time, artist and writer, Katherine Lesses wrote in an essay published by *Friends' Quarterly* in 1979 that long before she became a Quaker, she felt, "without being able to articulate it, that the practice of art I was engaging in was a spiritual exercise. From the time I began to attend [Friends] Meeting, I felt I had found a place where people were doing together what I had been doing alone" (134). Lesses observed that

> on the deepest level, art becomes a means of overcoming the separateness of one's existence, through sharing of an unseen world; and when art is concerned with the integration of experience, and the creation of form in relation to spiritual experience, then there is an interface between the function of art and religion in an individual's life, for both are concerned with finding underlying coherence and meaning. (133)

During that same period, Pleasaunce Holtom also heralded an opening to this sense of fresh illumination by calling other Quakers to "regard art not as an escape from reality, but as a manifestation of the Holy Spirit, whose power can shape our lives . . . as an instrument in our search for Truth" (1).

Likewise, Paul Eddington, a veteran British actor and a Quaker (a unique combination in the decade of the 1970s), made an observation concerning the obvious integration of his faith with his artistic vocation: "On the stage itself there is the constant attempt to simplify and to approach, even by only a little, an aspect of the Truth. Perhaps the theatre may seem to some an unexpected place in which to seek this sort of enlightenment, but are we not advised to be ready at all times to receive fresh light from whatever quarter it may come?" (16).

Throughout that period of awakening during the mid-twentieth century, Quakers were beginning to relate to art as an expression and prompter of their spiritual experience rather than primarily as a vice to draw their minds and hearts away from God and holy living. Thus, in his 1991 article "The Anti-Theatrical Prejudice Revisited," Michael Graves noted, "Today's Quakers are considerably less 'hard-shelled' and 'mole-eyed' [than the earlier description given by Jonas Barish] and there are signs on both sides of the Atlantic that the society of Friends has made progress toward making peace with the theatre" (1). Decidedly, threaded through the remarks of these contemporary Quaker scholars and artists is an emerging pattern borne of interweaving Art's potential transcendent nature into the fabric of Friends' belief and discipline. It seems Quakers could now recognize the arts, and particularly drama, for its potential as a channeled expression of their faith, rather than as a deviant deflector from fellowship with God.

~~~

As a drama director and university educator who is also a member of the Religious Society of Friends, I reflected on how an integration of Quaker principles naturally affected a consciously-defined behavior and attitude throughout the process of dramatic exploration and performance. After having directed more than 50 theatre productions and facilitated at least 15 traveling theatre ensembles along with various community and church drama events, I noted how my faith and practice were actually integral to the artistic collaborative process. It came quite naturally to me. I was drawn to develop a troupe of actors to create original dramatic vignettes to speak to issues of faith, social awareness, peace-making and community healing. We called ourselves Inter-Mission a Thinkable Theatre and functioned first out of George Fox College. The performances were initially created out of deep discussion and group reflection on current interpersonal and social concerns and then transformed into short provocative vignettes. Some of the themes dealt with fractures in communication, personal isolation, demoralizing institutionalization, artificial mask-wearing and role-playing, as well as societal pressure toward group think. While improvising with music, props, masks, mime and dialogue, the team attempted to explore ways of looking at and presenting revealed issues through performance. Without being overtly didactic or sermonizing, the performance pieces particularly capitalized on visual imagery and presentational theatricality with minimal verbiage. Since truth can be more gently slipped into a laughing mouth with an open mind, many of the pieces were dipped in tasteful humor. Others were performed in profound silence. As we recognized Jesus successfully used relevant story and parable to reveal Kingdom truths, we also went gently into rugged territory cloaked in metaphor and analogy, which produced perceptual shifts and a form of "aha" awareness. Thus, it was often called "thinkable theatre."

We created more than 300 short pieces that spoke to a variety of significant issues. Like Jesus, we were portable and flexible, able to pack a performance with a dozen pieces selected from the repertoire or create new ones for the needs of a particular group. The troupe then traveled easily, with only a trunk of props to perform at prisons, hospitals, schools, retreats, camps, care-homes, meetings and churches. We were always open for discussion, reflection and connection. Our direct verbal feedback and mail responses indicated that, while our audiences were theatrically entertained, they also often retained the content and intent of the creative presentations long after our departure. It was usually mentioned that the "seeds" of the presented concerns had indeed taken root. Consequently, respondents found themselves discussing the implications of the dramatic pieces in terms of their own conscience and altered awareness. Out of these experiences, I subsequently developed a course in Theatre Ministry on the George Fox College campus. The 1995 catalogue describes the course thus: "A consideration of theatre skills as tools for meeting human needs in essentially nontheatrical environments. Focus on drama as a service medium rather than as strictly an entertainment vehicle." The course continues to be listed in the George Fox University curriculum, although I am no longer on the faculty.

In terms of directing more traditional stage productions in a theatre in a college and community context, my Quaker sensitivities likewise informed their full purpose and process. I would spend many weeks researching dozens of drama scripts and praying over the final selections to determine which one merited the stewardship of time and effort (sometimes upwards to 200 hours within 4 to 8 weeks) from the performers and technical team during the process of collaborative creation. I believed the intention should also merit the time from the audience to participate in receiving the final gift of the production. While the play was always intended to be artistically tuned and theatrically viable for public presentation, I considered whether it would also become a vehicle for community growth and for deepening relationships within the cast as we worked to produce it. Likewise, would it be an opportunity for reflection and connection to spiritual truths for both the cast and the audience as they partook of the content? Furthermore, if the play never saw the joy and celebration of a final staged performance (which I considered was always a dire potential, although it rarely happened), would the extended process of creating it still have been good stewardship and worth the effort for the cast?

All of these concerns of course gave me pause and set me to a time of centering and waiting on the Spirit, both during the selection of the script, the casting of the actors, the engaging of the production team, the publication of the event, the presentation to the audience, and during a time of reflection with the cast afterwards. Apparent reciprocal rewards from the centering time spent on this process were experienced through a palpable joy discovered in building life-long relationships among the cast as well as with the recognition there was usually a minimal amount of interpersonal or technical conflict. While my process was satisfying, I discovered this style of directing is not necessarily universal even in other religious contexts, as some subsequent discussions with actors revealed. Some might find it relationally cumbersome and time-consuming, although I perceived it as worthy foundation building, which had a significant pay back. No productions were ever delayed and many were actually fine-tuned and ready for public presentation—often well in advance.

Therefore, while presenting many of the key Quaker concerns for spiritual life in the following section, I will concurrently note how they clearly can cast a certain guidance and illumination upon the Friendly director's, actor's and designer's motivations and actions, if they are mindful of using them. I also assert the practices are relevant to many other contexts outside theatre venues, such as mission and educational group projects. The principles likewise can become a powerful and positive template to work for more effective and healthy community process.

Since the bulwark of Friends' meeting for worship is centered in a desire to receive immediate inspiration and guidance from the Holy Spirit, the gathered fellowship is characterized by waiting in silence together for that spiritual "opening" and then acting or speaking in accordance with the leading when it has become clear. Many of the Quaker disciplines focus on a style of worship that celebrates waiting, looking inward, receiving inspiration and responding to spontaneous insight. Thus, those group behaviors would surely lead Quaker actors and directors to a comfort level with a theatre style that is based upon the sensitive listening and responding of each member. These attributes should be characteristic particularly of Creative Drama productions, ensemble improvisations, and role playing exercises, which depend primarily upon group interaction. However, most of the Quaker principles founded in their basic respect for the individuality of each member of the group and echoed in their notion that there is "that of God in every man," should have a direct impact on any theatre production involving Friends. The Quaker director's respect for the performers, the performers' mutual responsibility for the process and for self-preparation, and the notion of corporate centering for inspiration are among several key disciplines which would be immediately applicable to any venue of dramatic performance, whether "traditional" theatre dependent upon pre-scripted materials or "informal" theatre driven by creative improvisation. In fact, I also found them completely central to my own "theatre of the classroom" as an educator as well as during my roles as workshop and seminar facilitator.

In the following annotated list, I offer the parallels I have noticed between Quaker practice and the dramatic process. For the sake of focus, the guidelines at the beginning of each section are taken from the *Faith and Practice of New England Yearly Meeting of Friends (Book of Discipline)* which was adopted in 1985. These disciplines are typical of most yearly meetings of Friends throughout the world.

> • *When we gather together in worship let us remember that there is committed to each of us, as disciples of Christ, a share in the priesthood. We should help one another, whether in silence or through spoken prayer or words of ministry* (105).

The Quaker director likewise maintains an expectation in the performance ensemble that, as individuals, all are equal. While individual talent and personality vary, each has an equal position in community and, likewise, in ministry. Therefore, each is a support of the others and shared insight benefits the creation of the performed art.

> • *If the call comes, there should be no quenching of the spirit; the sense of our own unworthiness must not exempt us from this service, nor the fear of being unable to find the right words* (105). *A gathered meeting is no place for the enhancement of private reputations, but for self-effacing pliancy and obedience to the whispers of the Leader* (108).

In the creation of an artistic work, the Quaker director encourages and prompts the inspiration and input of each performer, recognizing that great insight may come through the seeming least of performers and that—when it does come and is revealed through inspired performance—it is a gift from above to be received and celebrated, but not to be lauded or revered as more worthy than that from others.

> • *Vocal messages can be as effective in a few halting but spiritually filled words as in the most learned and articulate message. . . Faithfulness in speaking, even very briefly, may open the way for fuller ministry from others. The tender and humble-*

minded utterance, given faithfully, can carry its message to the hearts of its hearers (105).

The Quaker director encourages the performers in improvised exercises to look inward and center on an inspiration or insight they may be receiving as they analyze a character or theme and then present it with confidence. Likewise, they must listen to and value the input of fellow performers with the expectation of receiving creative insight and imaginative material from them upon which they may build further to continue a theme or characterization. (I have also used role-play exercises in the classroom for similar purposes.)

> • *In the earliest period of the Christian Church His Spirit was, agreeable to ancient prophecy, poured upon servants and upon handmaidens; and we believe He continues to call from the young and from the old, from the unlearned and from the wise, from the poor and from the rich, from the women as well as from men. (106). No meeting can be held to the glory and in the power of God where His message, even through one of the weakest or most unattractive of his instruments, is suppressed* (111).

In the Quaker-driven theatre (or ministry), there should be no celebration of "star" performers or servility to directors or perceived prima donnas. Likewise, there should be equal recognition of technical personnel and other usually labeled "subservient" positions. All should have an equal voice for all are considered as "called" with the potential of being a vessel of creative insight.

> • *We do not regard those who have the gift of* ministry *as infallible . . . We feel that the gift is from above, and that on all of us lies the responsibility of being open to it, willing to receive it, should it be bestowed, and to use it faithfully while entrusted with it. But we fully recognize that to do this perfectly requires a continual submission of the will, and an unceasing watchfulness (106). Thus leadership in the meeting is widely shared, and the full body profits from that which each member can contribute* (110).

The Quaker director is not to consider him- or herself above the performers or staff, but rather a humble servant with the responsibility of a gift of leadership. It behooves the director to be a listener first and to be constant in prayer and intercession for the cast and crew as well as to be willing to share the apparent role of leadership when another appears to have a clear leading or insight concerning a matter at hand.

> • *True ministry comes from life . . .The Quaker group silence, the cooperative team work of the entire assembly . . . tend to heighten the spiritual quality of the person who rises in that kind of atmosphere to speak. But that group situation, important as it is, will not work the miracle of producing a message for the hour in a person who is sterile and has nothing to say. Even the miracle of feeding the multitude in Galilee needed at least a nucleus of loaves and fishes to start with . . .* (107).

The Quaker performers must accept the personal responsibility of preparing their hearts, minds, imaginations and bodies for the performance, as well as prior to all the rehearsals and meetings with the drama ensemble. While each may spontaneously draw upon the reserve of creative imagination in creating an ensemble piece, he or she cannot expect to draw deeply from a reservoir that is running dry from lack of input from observation, applied imagination, study or prayer. Likewise, all are expected to maintain well-nourished and exercised physical instruments, caring for their bodies and minds as the vehicles of expression for inspired performance.

> • *One never brings anything to meeting with the certainty of giving it there, but one tries not to come empty* (108).

The Quaker performer recognizes his or her responsibility as an active member of a community, one which requires the conscientious preparation and participation of each distinct part of the whole. He or she concentrates on the intention of the ensemble and therefore makes a concerted effort to locate materials, gather information and ponder the universal truths of the piece the group is constructing. The performers will not view themselves as a mere pawns in the hands of a director, to be moved about on the stage to create a satisfactory dramatic event, but will recognize their own spiritual responsibility to fill themselves in order to be poured out for the others.

> • *In the Meeting for Worship after the manner of Friends, it sometimes befalls that a person who feels moved to break the silence and share a fresh insight unknowingly expresses the thoughts of those listening. The speaker is not speaking to the Meeting; the gathered Meeting is speaking through one member* (110).

One must always remember that a dramatic production is a result of ensemble performance. As one speaks or acts, it is because he or she is in response, re-acting, to another. Each performer does not act in a vacuum, but as a significant part of the unified whole. Consequently, there are no small or insignificant parts.

> • *Simplicity is closely akin to sincerity—a genuineness of life and speech in which there is no place for sham or artificiality . . . . Care is needed to avoid and discourage the insincerities and extravagance that are prevalent in the social world . . . . We need also to speak the simple truth, in love, when occasion requires it* (144).

This discipline has distinct implications on the style in which a Quaker director works with an ensemble on a performance. He or she will take care to speak simply and truthfully when guiding the actors in performance, reflecting for them observations that can be understood and taken to heart for guidance and correction. In like manner, these practices will inform and direct the ensemble in the creation and selection of artistic pieces that fulfill the obligation to speak the truth in love, free of meaningless sham. It will also undergird them in financial decision-making and technical design.

> • *Friends should promote high standards of quality and moral influence in all forms of entertainment . . . . Friends seek to live in the world, to be a part of it, and to be a leaven to its standards of daily conduct and custom* (145).

This discipline has direct and pointed implications on the process and the product of theatre. Therefore, the selection process in the preparation for performance is not entered into lightly. The motivation for all who are involved in producing the event is carefully considered. The apparent needs and concerns expressed in the community of believers, as well as the community of participants, and the anticipated community of spectators are a matter of meditation for insight. Waiting in prayer for a leading to the most expedient material for performance is a crucial first step to the entire process. A concern for wise investment of the time needed to process a performance leads directors and producers to select materials and themes for artistic expression that are transcendent, seek universal truth, and speak to the hearts and minds of those concerned, whether on stage or in audiences. The workman's skill, dedication, commitment and integrity are reflected in the quality of his or her work. Finally, quality work, which reflects the dedication and love of the artist, blesses the receiver. The intention for the Quaker director and actor is for the receiver to be moved by the presentation, rather than for the performer to garner the glory—and for the performer to be changed by the process rather than be prostituted for the product.

~~~

Having looked at these principles of faith and practice of Friends and the potential to exhibit parallel values in creative drama, I turn now to relating some instances of awakening to those very possibilities. On the American front, Quaker groups primarily expressed their support of theatre through their college drama programs. In addition to regular traditional theatre seasons, they saw drama as an educational and evangelistic tool, as well as a fundamental expression of the liberal and communicative arts. In keeping with their commitment to community, during the decades of the 1970s and 1980s, some American Quaker colleges developed touring theatre companies such as *Friendship Seven* and *Inter-Mission* (mentioned earlier) and University Players as tools for outreach and ministry. Robust theatre programs exist today in most Quaker educational institutions. Whether they mindfully utilize Friends guidelines for faith and practice in their productions can only be discovered on an individual basis. While there does not appear to be a plethora of material on this topic, a provocative article by Bryan Boyd titled "Quaker Corporate Discernment as a Model for Collaboration in Theatre" does indicate that at least Boyd, as a theatre designer and educator on the George Fox University faculty, was indeed prompted by his Quaker faith and practice within his production teams.

The remainder of this paper, however, will focus primarily upon the British Quaker applications of the dramatic arts because they were directly sponsored by the denomination itself, the London Yearly Meeting of the Society of Friends.

During the decade of the 1970s Hugh Pyper noted that several factors contributed to the dramatic burst of energy that instigated the use of drama as a medium of communication among Friends. He stated:

> In Britain as a whole, concern over peace issues has been growing as international tensions increase. This has been matched by a renewed awareness by peace workers of the potency of drama, particularly street theatre, as a way of catching and holding people's attention. People who would walk past the most carefully displayed bookstall may be induced to stop, listen, and think by the sight of six skeletons carrying a coffin. (596)

Two national vehicles for drama within London Quaker Yearly Meeting emerged during this period. These were called *Quaker Peace Action Caravan* and the *Quaker Youth Theatre*, also known as *The Leaveners*. *The Leaveners'* first official appearance was at the residential Yearly Meeting in Lancaster in 1978 where the troupe worked for a week on street theatre sketches to present at various sites around the city throughout the festival.

It is significant to note that in early seventeenth-century Quaker history, the city of Lancaster was a place of suffering where many Friends were imprisoned for the convictions of their faith. Therefore, in 1978 when the London Yearly Meeting of Friends was to hold their Quaker Festival in Lancaster, there was a particular response to the realization that, for the first time in centuries, they would be back in the historical city in large numbers, but would now be free to express their beliefs. They thought that surely there must be some "sign" to be given in Lancaster. Much of that sign was actually delivered through theatrical presentations. Peter Whittle observed

> Where Friends had suffered Friends were now offering fun and laughter in exchange, both the ancient suffering and the present joy springing from the same convictions. It was much easier to hold a small placard saying, 'I'm a Friend' than to lie in a prison cell in Lancaster castle, but it was good to be able to express one's gratitude for being able to do the former rather than be called upon to endure the latter. (Whittle 235)

The Leaveners Theatre Troupe worked for the week prior to that culminating festival with a group of about forty young people to create a theatrical expression to be shared with all participants of the conference: A Nuclear Dragon. Peter Whittle stated that the dragon

> not only caught the imagination of those who worked upon it, but taught us something about our attitude towards power . . . *Now* we build our own dragons in the shape of nuclear weapons. The children understood something of this imagery to the extent of realizing that sophisticated weapons, like our own dragon, demand a great deal of devotion in the making and some intelligence and skill, and can be admired even while they are detested for what they represent. (236)

The "performance" was staged throughout the city—in front of the castle where early Quakers had been imprisoned, in the Gardens, at the Park on the grass and in the rain. Whittle explained that a crowd of about 2,000 gathered to participate with the performers and "when the wind blew away the words, Friends considered that place where words came from" (235).

Following Friends' tradition, the leaflets received by the audience simply said they "would know" when it was the end of the meeting. In the case of the festival—after waiting for that *sense* of closure—balloons were released in a final and dramatic act in celebration of their freedom. It is now apparent that in the conception, planning and development process for the event in Lancaster, the Quaker artists involved in leadership directly and intuitively applied many of the very principles I have mentioned earlier in this text. They clearly valued the input of the "least" among them. They valued the spiritual message as it emerged through one of the weakest or most unattractive of instruments, "even to the equal standing of children as young as five years of age." Likewise, they sought to "speak the simple truth in love" and were received in that spirit as well.

The experience in Lancaster proved so rewarding and memorable that the following year in Newcastle, more than fifty young people spent a week putting together a two-and-one-half-hour musical play that was written, cast, choreographed and performed in public at a local theatre. *The Quest of the Golden Eye* was "based on Persian mythology, but conveyed an essentially Quaker message, so that not only did young Friends have to work through the dilemmas posed by the dramatic situations, but a stock of lively dramatic material which other groups could use began to accumulate" (Pyper 598).

As one young Friend, Vicki Jewell, recalled, "they fitted the play round the actors, rather than doing the more usual fitting of the actors to the play" (qtd. in Pyper 235). This kind of treatment of the performers and the fleshing out of the theme is again characteristic of Quaker sensitivity to corporate worship and the notion that the process, the experience, is as important as the product – and sometimes more so.

In numerous subsequent performances, the Leaveners worked with upwards to 150 people in week-long projects to create original pieces for public sharing. Alec Davison remarked about the minor miracle of creating the impossible in a week because of its very Quakerly-ness in the way of working with people:

> The performers . . . bubble over in a *peaceable* explosion of creativity and affirmation that enheartens their supporters and in turn re-*quickens* their own enthusiasm. Here is a *sparking of the spirit* that is profoundly Quakerly and yet which would have made our forefathers shake with confusion . . . . Many will have known *new openings* as they made themselves vulnerable and raw to the *spirit's working* and in the acceptance and love that this generates they will have fused friendships of new depths: for a moment they have tasted what a society of friends might be about. They are very close to that spirit experienced by early Friends when they suffered together to *publish the truth*. (243)

I note the inculcation of certain Quaker terminology which is usually descriptive of Quaker worship, but which is used here by Davison to enthusiastically describe their "dramatic" experience as parallel to a spiritual one. "In addition people accepted each other in a Quakerly fashion—respected them for what they were without reservations." Others noted, "It is Quakerly in the way it is organised, the way decisions are arrived at, the importance accorded to worship . . . the earthy directness" (244).

These responses of the participants can be laid to the style of leadership that naturally inculcates Quaker principles into the process. This is reflected in the following observation made by Davison, who evaluated the proceedings:

> Great stress is laid throughout the week on group work and shared responses; this helps to mitigate against the star system and theatrical camp. Instead, a sincerity of acting is encouraged that may lack technique but comes from having been involved in the development of the thinking and the issues. For drama is essentially about moral education in action, about characters in tense or desperate or farcical situations who have to make choices and decisions. The group soon rejects what is phony or over the top or imposed and, in this way, resists manipulation. The company at its general and annual gatherings asks to work on themes that are meaty and rich in sustenance but which are not preachy or strongly ideological. (246)

The Leaveners have taken a serious interest in their mission to speak to the current social issues and invest themselves in the development of young Friends through the medium of creative drama. In their Spring 1991 newsletter, the scope of their vision and the dimensions of their creativity are obvious in the descriptions of the venues for one year alone. Their open invitation to participation includes the following notices:

- In Bradford, we will physically build our own city of visions. Using music, dance, drama, large puppets and masks, we will bring this city to life in the light of the day and the dark of the night. We will look back at early Quaker visions and find our own vision of the future where people and faiths can find a way to lasting peace.
- As our contribution in a multitude of national and international events planned by Oxfam to use the year to address issues of world poverty, the Leaveners proposed a multiple venture that would engage theatre as a way of consciousness-raising.
- Work on a Theatre-Go-Round style project centered on issues of Health Education to be taken to schools and children's homes in Romania.

• Devising a show which gives insights to life in Moscow. The show includes a soundtrack, slides of Sergei's life and family, and can be extended into a full day's drama workshop. (Sergei is apparently a fictional Russian "Everyman" character.)
• (Developing) an international team . . . to go clowning about in Northern Ireland.
• "Confronting Conflict: Playing with Fire"—a multi-week educational workshop program including mask work which focuses on Persecutor, Rescuer and Victim. During the final three weeks the group took their Playing with Fire workshop to the North London Education Project, a housing and education project for ex-offenders; to a residential training weekend for youth workers and to a school for boys with emotional behavioural difficulties. (*Leavenings*, Spring 1991)

The Leaveners have been the most prolific and ongoing of the British Quaker drama projects. However, for a sojourn during the decade of the 1970s and briefly into the 1980s, a project known as the *Quaker Peace Action Caravan* was functioning along-side *The Leaveners*, but with a specific agenda. Q-PAC was a troupe of touring Friends whose aim and objectives focused on working for a less violent world. The *Quaker Peace Action Caravan* traveled throughout the British Isles, performing wherever they had opportunity. This included each of the seventy-two Monthly Meetings, schools, County Shows and even at the launching of the World Disarmament Campaign.

"Dramaquest" was one of the activities of *Questabout*—a branch of *England's Children* and *Young People's Committee* demonstrating its concern for the youth in the Society of Friends in a very positive and constructive way. The program utilized local workshops and link groups, which studied issues of social and spiritual concern, using a variety of group process methods—including dramatic role-play—to gain empathy and a deeper understanding of the people and the issues.

One such *DramaQuest* event was described by John Anderson as having taken place at various locations around Swarthmoor Hall, near Lancaster. Young people were engaged in creating improvised scenes depicting the early history of the Quaker movement as it began to show itself at Swarthmoor Hall in 1652. The background of the episode was discussed and the important figures were presented to the young people involved in the historical exploration. Five situations were examined in groups outside on the lawn of the great hall. Then the episodic play began with each group presenting their piece of the unfolding puzzle in the actual location of the historical event. The performance moved from site to site with audience and performers moving into the new location with a brief narrative transition afforded in route.

Accordingly, the scenes were enacted upon the front lawn, in the entry hall, in Margaret Fell's bedroom (with the four-poster bed serving as the central *stage* for the action), in the famous dining hall where the Friends' first Meeting for Worship actually took place, in Judge Fell's parlour, and finally in the attic "that may have once accommodated forty-odd Parliamentarian troopers."

Anderson's observations of the theatrical process and the students' responses noted that:

> Any watcher must have been deeply impressed by the spirit they had all shown, by the gusto with which each had entered into his or her part and put that part into the group's play. Little self-consciousness was shown; rather was seen a deep consciousness of their environment and what had happened there. And by their words and deeds they showed a genuine understanding of events and their significance, and in all a happy seriousness. (225)

The Leaveners and its various branches continue to promote Quaker values through the arts, functioning out of a permanent location in Birmingham, England. They are recognized as a relevant social resource, receiving support from family and friends, yearly meetings, substantial patrons and as a member of The National Council for Voluntary Youth Service. Their websites and publications indicate they create and promote projects and educational events that "explore issues relating to human rights, social justice, peace and spirituality." These include poetry, music and art, as well as drama and debate workshops. For example, their current DramaQuest features a two-day workshop that focuses on children "who have been real heroes in history," including present-day children who have become active in fighting the wars of slavery and poverty. Other pertinent recent endeavors include such titles as: "Doing the Right Thing" (a drama workshop centered in exploring conscientious objection), "Militarisation Drama and Music Workshop" at Hereford Meeting, a "Does Slavery Still Exist" workshop, and "Conflict Resolution" drama workshops at Wimbledon meeting. The latter utilized the story of Ferdinand the Bull "to explore both historical and contemporary conflict resolution issues. The drama and music activities offered space for both moral reflection and fun. The themes that arose shed light on both historical and contemporary conflict resolution issues. As one participant stated: 'The story itself, and added scenes about Gandhi, Nazi Germany and modern school bullying, had more depth & spiritual depth than I had expected'" (*Leaveners*).

Certainly, there are numerous Quaker historical productions, including a one-person show on Mary Dyer, called "Mary's Joy" currently playing in the United States. There are also various Friendly venues, such as The Fellowship of Quakers in the Arts, housed in Philadelphia Yearly Meeting. Undoubtedly there are significant theatrical productions that support spiritual values presented in Quaker schools, colleges and universities across the nation. These all merit further research for future publications, beyond the scope of this current essay.

Finally, in terms of Quakers and their historical distrust of the theatre, perhaps many of the mentioned experiences with creative drama and its impact upon the community may help to view Friends in a fresh, new light and soften the vastly generalized Quaker suspicion toward theatre. However, one still maintains that a good measure of reticence should indeed be expected of a society that sees itself as being called to address issues of cultural darkness with purposeful light and leaven. I hope there continues to be a healthy concern and robust discussion about the wholesale negativity, abuse and violence seen in a considerable amount of contemporary films and the media—with a decided Quaker stand against such. Likewise, perhaps some dyed-in-the-gray-wool Quakers, who are hesitant to unequivocally embrace all the dramatic arts, may now be more inclined to recognize a certain form of "User-Friendly Theatre." That is, consider and produce live theatre that brings light into the darkness and clearly reflects the Quaker principles of "community" throughout the entire process of its preparation, while speaking to the specific *needs* of the community in the purpose of its presentation.

✳ Works Cited ✳

Anderson, John. "What is 'Dramaquest'?" *Quaker Monthly*. 65-11 (1986): 222-225. Print.

Barclay, Robert. *An Apology for the True Christian Divinity* . . . . 1678. 13th ed. Manchester, England: William Irwin, 1869. Print.

Barnes, Kenneth C. *The Creative Imagination* . Swarthmore Lecture, 1960. London: George Allen & Unwin, 1960. Print.

Barish, Jonas. *The Anti-theatrical Prejudice*. Berkeley, CA: U of California, 1981. Print.

Benner, John. "Art and So On." *Quaker Monthly*. 59-12 (1980): 233-236. Print.

Blamires, David. "Traditional Quakers Challenged." *Quaker Monthly*. 57-9 (1978): 161-164. Print.

Book of Discipline of New York Yearly Meeting of the Religious Society of Friends, General Conference Affiliation. Rev. ed. New York: Knickerbocker, 1930. Print.

Book of Discipline of Ohio Yearly Meeting of the Friends Church. Rev.ed. Damascus,

Ohio, 1968. Print.

Boyd, Bryan. "Quaker Corporate Discernment as a Model for Collaboration in Theatre" *George Fox University.edu* PDF - 209.170.248.51 (ND) Web.

Coren, Pamela. "Quakers and the ArtsAgain." *Quaker Monthly.* 67-7 (1988): 150-151. Print.

Davison, Alec. "Effervescence from the Leaveners." *The Friends' Quarterly.* 23 (1984): 243-248. Print.

Eddington, Paul. "Actor and Friend." *Quaker Monthly.* 59-1 (1980): 14-16. Print.

Eversley, Ruth. "Living with the Quaker Peace Action Caravan." *Quaker Monthly.* 62-1 (1983): 12-15. Print.

Faith and Practice of New England Yearly Meeting of Friends (Book of Discipline). N. p.: New England Yearly Meeting of Friends, 1985. Print.

Foreman, Connie. "A Senior Citizen' at Her First Yearly Meeting." *Quaker Monthly* . 57-11 (1978): 204-206. Print.

Foster, Richard. "How Liberating are the Liberal Arts?" *Evangelical Friend.* Jan/Feb, 1988: 8-10. Print.

Gilderdale, Alan. "The Position of the Artist in the Society of Friends." *The Friends' Quarterly* . 19 (1976): 325-330. Print.

Graves, Michael. "The Anti-Theatrical Prejudice Revisited: A Late Twentieth Century Quaker Perspective," a paper presented at the Association for Theatre in Higher Education Convention, Seattle, Washington, August 1991, subsequently published in *Truth's Bright Embrace:Essays and Poems in Honor of Arthur O. Roberts.* Edited by Paul N. Anderson and Howard R. Macy. George Fox University Press, 1996. Print.

Greenwood, J. Ormerod. *Signs of Life: Art and Religious Experience* . Swarthmore Lecture, 1978. London: Quaker Home Service, 1978. Print.

Holden, John. "The Necessity of Art." *Quaker Monthly.* 59-5 (1980): 89-91. Print.

Holtom, Pleasaunce. "Young Makers." *Quaker Monthly.* 55-1 (1976): 1-4. Print.

Jewell, Vicki. "The *Golden Eye* at Newcastle." *Quaker Monthly.* 58-12 (1979): 234-235. Print.

"The Leaveners Rise Again." *Quaker Monthly.* 58-6 (1983): 110. Print.

Leaveners: Inspiring Change through the Arts. Web. 11 Aug. 2015. <www.leaveners.org>.

Leavenings: A Termly Newsletter of the Leaveners—The Quaker Performing Arts Project. London: Leaveners Arts Base, Spring, 1991. Print.

Lerner, Laurence. *The Two Cinnas: Quakerism, Revolution and Poetry.* Swarthmore Lecture, 1984. London: Quaker Home Service, 1984. Print.

Lesses, Katherine. "Art and Integration." *The Friends' Quarterly.* 21 (1979): 128-137. Print.

Marsh, John. "The LeavenersAn Appraisal." *The Friends' Quarterly* . 25 (1988): 56-61. Print.

Nicholson, Frederick J. *Quakers and the Arts: A Survey of Attitudes of British Friends to the Creative Arts from the Seventeenth to the Twentieth Century.* London: Friends Home Service Committee, 1968. Print.

Palmer, Candida. "Cultural Impedimenta Old and New in Friends' Relation to the Arts: Some Preliminary Reflections." *Quaker Religious Thought.* 14 (1972-73): 2-26.

Penn, William. *No Cross, No Crown.* London,1682. Print.

Principles of Quakerism: A Collection of Essays. Issued by the representatives of the Religious Society of Friends for Pennsylvania, New Jersey and Delaware. Philadelphia, 1908. Print.

Pyper, Hugh. "Witnessing for Peace: The Drama of Peace." *The Friends' Quarterly.* 22 (1982): 596-598. Print.

Rowntree, John Stephenson. *Quakerism: Past and Present.* London: Smith & Elder, 1859. Print.

Rules of Discipline of the Yearly Meeting of Friends of North Carolina. Woodland, NC, 1908. Print.

Sharman, Alison. "Leaven and Fire." *Quaker Monthly.* 61-12 (1982): 249-250. Print.

Shepherd, Jack. *Makepeace Daly's Street Theatre.* London: Quaker Home Service, 1986. Print.

Whittle, Peter. "A Quaker Demo." *Quaker Monthly.* 57-12 (1978): 234-236. Print.

Windle, Barbara. "Lerner Meets Laurence Meets Lerner." *QuakerMonthly* . 63-8 (1984): 153-156. Print.

Autobiography as Spiritual Opportunity:
This Speaks to My Condition

by Mike Heller

We have an affinity for life stories. I remember listening to my father at the kitchen table telling about the time his B-29 crashed in the Pacific, and half of the crew died. The plane hit the water just after dark. It broke in two on the first impact with the waves, and the final impact drove the nose underwater. My father got out of his escape hatch with difficulty, swam to the surface, and came up under the torn steel of the wing which cut his head. The radio and radar operators pulled him into an inflatable life raft, and then pulled the bombardier in. The co-pilot sat on the wing, which rolled with the waves, and threatened to puncture the raft. He fended off the raft with his foot. "Get in the raft," one of the men yelled. Seeing that the right gunner was caught inside, the co-pilot dove off the wing and swam to a break in the fuselage. As he disappeared inside, the plane suddenly sank and they had no time to get out. The navigator and tail gunner had escaped on the other side of the plane but their life raft failed to inflate. One of the gunners in a life jacket had escaped, too, but he got separated from them and drifted off, never to be seen again. My father and the three other guys in the life raft floated alone on a rough sea. The waves broke over them all night. At the end of the next day, they were picked up by a destroyer escort. A short time later the ship picked up the navigator and tail gunner, too.

This event, late in World War II, had profound effects on my father. I can't say he loved the Air Force, but it had a strong hold on him. He ended up staying in the Air Force for a career. Therefore, I grew up on airbases. People are surprised to learn that I graduated from West Point, served in the Army, then became a Quaker. After graduation, I went on to Ranger School, where I carried an M-16 and a seventy-pound rucksack. We got so worn out that one time or another each of us fell asleep on our feet slogging through the rain. Apparently my mild demeanor goes against people's expectations of Army Rangers. They wonder if I was a Quaker at the time (I wasn't). If truth be known, it's partly because of that mild demeanor that I wasn't cut out for an Army officer's life. Enough people asked me how all of this happened that I realized there is a story here that I might be able to write.

I turned away from the Army – not to become a John Woolman or Dorothy Day, or an extraordinary nonviolent social activist – but to become a teacher of literature and peace studies. There's a line of development from being in the Army, to becoming a Quaker, to becoming a teacher of literature. I have come to see how my teaching draws upon Quaker-inspired values. Although it's too much to claim that my teaching represents a Quaker pedagogy of literary study, the process of reading and responding that I have developed with my students is based upon framing values expressed in the Quaker way of worship. This essay describes this Quaker-inspired learning process as I see it shaping my teaching of spiritual autobiographies.[1]

Autobiography as a Spiritual Opportunity

In a course that I recently taught, called "Nonviolence as a Spiritual Journey," we focused on four spiritual autobiographies that provide a broad perspective on nonviolent activism: John Woolman's *Journal*, Mohandas K. Gandhi's *Autobiography*, Dorothy Day's *The Long Loneliness*, and Marian Wright Edelman's *Lanterns: A Memoir of Mentors*. These books stimulate thinking about

---

[1] For their help on the present essay, many thanks to Ivan Brownotter, Katherine Hoffman, and Robert Morris.

My deep appreciation to members of our "Nonviolence as a Spiritual Journey" course – Jessica Compton, Wes Knowles, John Lilley, Alejandro Menjivar, Rachel Miles, Kayleigh Murphy, Daniel Osborne, and Kelsey Reedy – for all that they brought of themselves to our course. They each gave me permission to quote from their course writings. Jessica, Wes, Daniel, and Kelsey presented papers from our course at Virginia Tech's 2015 symposium "Cultivating Peace: A Student Research Symposium on Violence Prevention."

Details of the B-29 crash are taken from two documents: a memo my father wrote to the Casualty Branch of the War Department in November 1945 and a letter he wrote in June 2001 in response to an inquiry about the pilot Lt. Henry Mellen.

I tell more of my story in "From West Point to Quakerism," Pendle Hill Pamphlet 389 (Wallingford, PA: Pendle Hill Publications, April 2007).

the lives of each of these nonviolent social activists, the historical context of their times, issues of reading autobiographical narratives, and aspects of our own lives. Perhaps social justice issues are always rooted in life stories.

There are multiple ways we can read texts like these – an historical approach, close reading, Marxist readings, psychoanalytic readings, and so on – all of which we touched on in the course. I sought a holistic approach, so I asked students to keep a personal journal and share with the class Small Writings, which are brief personal narratives from their lives and which in some ways are similar to messages spoken in a Quaker Meeting. We had conversations about each book, and we reflected on what we each brought to the reading. I was not aiming for students to leave the course as committed social activists, but I wanted them to think about nonfiction and autobiography. I wanted them to think about personal qualities such as humility, compassion, perseverance, and sacrifice, which are evident in the lives of these social activists.[2]

Bill Tabor, a much-admired teacher at Pendle Hill, used to say that each one-on-one meeting with a student is a spiritual opportunity. Reading these autobiographies is a kind of spiritual opportunity, too. I am borrowing from Quaker ideals, but I want our study of these autobiographies to go beyond any particular faith. I believe that our work has a spiritual dimension. Unlike George Fox and John Woolman, I am not concerned with speaking in class from a direct experience of the inward Spirit. Rather, I am asking students to think about what they can say from their experience of reading and reflecting on their lives. I am asking them to speak from their hearts as well as their minds, and to consider how the inward life helps to direct one's outward life. Students can come from any faith or none, but wherever they are with faith, I am interested.

We asked how important faith is to nonviolent activism. That question led us to consider the role of faith in the American Civil Rights movement as well as the ideas of recent theorists, such as Gene Sharp, who question its necessity for effective nonviolent activism (Cortright 77). I welcomed students' questions and skepticism about the extent to which nonviolence can be effective. In his *Autobiography*'s Introduction, Gandhi says that Truth is God and God is Truth ("I worship God as Truth only. I have not yet found Him, but I am seeking after Him" [ix]). One of the students, Kelsey, offered a healthy skepticism to this discussion because she was not drawn to spiritual expressions, but she was

---

[2] I talk about teaching with Small Writings in "'Wait to Be Gathered': The Classroom as Spiritual Place" in *Minding the Light: Essays in Friendly Pedagogy*, eds. Anne Dalke and Barbara Dixson (NY: Peter Lang, 2004) 43-63.

deeply moved to serve others. She could see the value in Woolman writing about the dangers of wanting too much to please people. Kelsey wrote about the importance of a distinction made by Woolman about "learning with the end of pleasing men and learning in order to please God (a word which we might interpret to be synonymous with universal love, justice, or peace)." She substituted for God the terms that speak to her condition: "universal love, justice, and peace." Several students expressed appreciation for the emphasis of our course on both the inward and outward life. Kelsey quoted Woolman warning his readers against "tutors [who] are not acquainted with sanctification of spirit, nor experienced in an humble waiting for the leadings of truth, but follow the maxims of wisdom of this world" (85). And then she added, "I think this quote goes right along with . . . [the idea] that teachers too frequently focus on the outward life of a student, forgetting that students have inward needs and much personal growth to attend to on an emotional and, perhaps we might say, spiritual level." Kelsey helped us question the relation between faith and social action. She represented the significant number of young people who do not define faith in traditional spiritual terms but want to serve others.

"This I Knew Experimentally"

When I was still in the army I attended my first Quaker meeting. I was captivated by what happened in the hour of silent worship. At first my thoughts flew rapidly by like fishing line zinging off the reel. I lost track of how much time passed. After experiencing my whirring mind, that first burst of inward awareness, the thoughts slowed. I gradually became aware of the people sitting in silence around me. I heard a young person in a nearby pew stand and speak about love in a deeply heartfelt way. After a period of silence another person spoke, and then after more silence, another. I sensed intuitively the important value Quakers placed on the experience of one's inward life. It was this unprogrammed worship, framed by silence, and its inward drama that first attracted me. Although my army experience helped create in me a readiness to learn about nonviolence, it was the experience of the silent worship that first attracted me.

George Fox, in his *Journal*, explains a major turning point in his life that marked the beginning of the Quaker movement. As a young man, he was in inner turmoil, walking from town to town in northwest England, in the late 1640s, trying to find a priest who could help him. The realization he came to would be central to the founding of the Quaker faith: "I saw that there was none among them all that could speak to my condition. And when all my hopes in them and in all men were gone. . . . I heard a voice which said, 'There is one, even Christ Jesus, that can speak to thy condition. . . . And this I knew *experimentally*" (11, italics added). Fox's statement looks back on the beginnings of the Quaker movement and establishes the importance of knowing "experimentally." Quakerism became known as an "experimental" or "experiential" faith.

Another expression of experience's meaning comes from Isaac Penington, in 1661, who tells his readers that the inward Spirit is found in the surrender of one's own willing efforts:

> Give over thine own willing; give over thine own running; give over thine own desiring to know or to be any thing, and sink down to the seed which God sows in the heart, and let that grow in thee, and be in thee, and breathe in thee, and act in thee, and thou shalt find by sweet *experience* that the Lord knows that, and loves and owns that, and will lead it to the inheritance of life, which is his portion.

Penington emphasizes the necessity of yielding to the paradoxically passive action of giving over.

Woolman's and Gandhi's autobiographies are experiential records. Knowing "experimentally" or through "experience" is key to the holistic knowing that these books are all about. Although I put less emphasis on surrender and yielding to the Spirit than Woolman, the process I am emphasizing encourages students to value their inward experience. As Mary Conrow Coelho writes, "We know life and the world from within" (21). At the beginning of our course, I ask students to keep a personal journal, and I say, "We are on a two-fold journey, an inward journey into ourselves and an outward journey into the world. Watch what happens for you with both of these journeys." Mary Rose O'Reilley talks about this in *Radical Presence: Teaching as Contemplative Practice*:

> Theorists . . . have explored the idea, should a theoretical foundation be needed, that students *have* an inner life and that its authority is central to understanding cognitive development . . . . Some pedagogical practices crush the soul; most of us have suffered their bruising force. Others allow the spirit to come home: to self, to community, and to the revelations of reality. (3)

When I first read her book, I found support for what I felt drawn to. Mary Rose, with a touch of humor, sees teachers as somewhat like Zen masters: "I see my colleagues practicing this patient discernment as seriously as any Zen master, though they may call it simply draft conferencing" (3). Reading and responding to literature involves a sensitivity to what comes to each of us from our inward life—reading comes from and leads to our inner life.

Woolman's *Journal* represents a particularly Quaker idea of experiential writing. He begins his *Journal* by writing, "I have often felt a motion of love to leave some hints in writing of my experience of the goodness of God, and now, in the thirty-sixth year of my age, I begin this work" (5). This use of a semi-passive verb structure ("I have often felt a motion of love") expresses a life of yielding to the Spirit felt within. His *Journal* takes on these stylistic qualities to emphasize his experience of God working in his life. Although Quakers called these books Journals, they are a kind of spiritual autobiography, written and revised for publication, with the purpose of strengthening the spiritual life of his community. As my friend Rebecca Mays has shared in discussions about the Quaker journal tradition, these books have a mirroring quality. Quakers expected these journals to invite readers into reflecting on their own experience.

Gandhi's *Autobiography*, which has the subtitle *My Experiments with Truth*, represents another doorway for discussing the importance of experience. The term "Experiments" suggests the scientist's idea of testing an hypothesis, but also it suggests knowledge that is based on experience. Gandhi could just as well have subtitled the book "My Experience with Truth." His *Autobiography* offers numerous topics for discussion and reflection that connect with students' own experiences. Gandhi writes how he tried smoking cigarettes and eating meat, how he and a friend played with the idea of committing suicide (a passage that my students found very upsetting), and how he stole gold from his brother and made a confession to his father, which Gandhi says was a major lesson in his early life. He writes that

> This was, for me, an object-lesson in Ahimsa . . . . A clean confession, combined with a promise never to commit the sin again, when offered before one who has the right to receive it, is the purest type of repentance. I know that my confession made my father feel absolutely safe about me, and increased his affection for me beyond measure. (24)

When Gandhi went to London and law school he tried to become an English gentleman by taking elocution, dancing, and violin lessons, but he finally realized that he was wasting his time. Our class had heated discussions about Gandhi's experiments with diet, his criticism of the Eiffel Tower as serving no useful purpose, and his confessions about failing in his efforts to educate his sons. Students were upset at how he treated his wife Kasturbai. Based on the

Autobiography, they argued that he was a terrible husband, an interpretation which required us to consider evidence from other sources.

I asked the class to look at Gandhi's chapter "Shyness My Shield," because it spoke to me about my own shyness and I assumed it would speak to many students. While in London for law school, the college-age Gandhi became active in the vegetarian club – an empowering experience in an organization, much like that of our students becoming active in a campus club or organization. This seemingly small commitment was a steppingstone to his becoming a great leader. In this chapter, he tells the story of how he invited his vegetarian friends to a dinner on the night before his departure for India. When he stood to make his prepared speech, however, he was paralyzed by shyness and could only say one sentence of thanks to his friends. The story is remarkable not only because he will go on to become such an articulate speaker and leader, but also because in retrospect he discovers that this shyness is in fact a strength. At the end of the chapter, Gandhi says, "My shyness has been in reality my shield and buckler. It has allowed me to grow. It has helped me in my discernment of truth" (55). This chapter provided an opportunity to think about our own hidden strengths. I wanted us to watch for useful metaphors that are suggestive for thinking about our own lives (such as "Shyness my Shield").

Students in our class wrote about the ways these books touched their personal lives. Jessica read the *Journal* as Woolman intended it, as a way to reflect on her own experience. Jessica discovered that she had a common experience with Edelman's *Lanterns* and thought about the importance of family in her life. She and Edelman both grew up in South Carolina: "Even though Edelman's background is different from my own," Jessica writes, "we share many of the values that she developed in her formative years that shaped her calling." She was interested in how "Edelman was surrounded by a family who not only cared deeply about her, but also challenged her to live a life of Christian faith and academic excellence" (5). She felt many similarities to her own experience of receiving scholarships, studying abroad, and gaining self-confidence. "When her time abroad came to an end," Jessica writes, Edelman "did not return home the same person who had left. The new wine of freedom and self-confidence could not be poured back into the old wineskin of the Jim Crow South or into the traditional confines of what a Black woman could aspire to in America" (45). Jessica then speaks of her own life:

> Like Edelman, I grew up in South Carolina, my Christian faith has always profoundly influenced the way I act and treat other people, and I pride myself on doing my best academically. I have had many of the

same incredible international travel opportunities that have transformed my perspective on the world in college, and I have a heart that is enflamed by today's social injustices. Despite our differences, all of these similarities made it easy for me to compare myself to Edelman, relate to her struggles, and take much of her advice to heart when I read her memoir.

She concludes by saying she feels challenged by Edelman to pursue her own calling as an educator and to be a mentor to young people. Jessica went on the next semester to develop an outstanding curriculum on peace and justice studies for high school students.

The autobiography writers in our course challenged accepted social constructs. Through their life's work and their writing, these social activists resisted the accepted norms, shifted them, and changed how we see them. Gandhi created a fusion, in his own terms, of Hinduism, Islam, and Christianity. He loved the Sermon on the Mount and learned to redefine opponents as friends. He challenges us as readers to think about how we can do this, too.

Autobiography and Experience (A Little Theory)

Quaker worship, spiritual autobiography, and much American poetry share the central importance of experience. In the mid-1840s, Ralph Waldo Emerson spoke of experience in a way that answered to his time and place, as American writers looked for a literature that would express the potential of a new democratic nation on the world stage. Emerson called for a poet who would write from his (or her) own experience in a way that would represent the new American nation: "The poet has a new thought; he has a whole new experience to unfold; he will tell us how it was with him, and all men will be the richer in his fortune. For, the experience of each new age requires a new confession, and the world seems always waiting for its poet" (225). A decade later, Walt Whitman answered this call with *Leaves of Grass*, his ambitious, autobiographical masterpiece, in which he too makes spiritual claims. In "Song of Myself," Canto 5, Whitman writes of mystical knowing:

> Swiftly arose and spread around me the peace and knowledge that pass all the argument of the earth,
> And I know that the hand of God is the promise of my own,
> And I know that the spirit of God is the brother of my own,
> And that all the men ever born are also my brothers, and the women my sisters and lovers,
> And that a keelson of the creation is love. . . . (33)

QUAKERS AND THE DISCIPLINES

Whitman's impulse is democratic and Romantic, in that he tries to encompass, speak for, and validate the experience of all people of every race and class. For Emerson and Whitman, experience was complex, difficult, and evolving. Before Emerson wrote "The Poet" and the words above about experience, his son Waldo had died of scarlet fever in January 1842. He was heartbroken and his faith was shaken. He no longer had the confidence that he expressed in "The American Scholar." After "The Poet," he wrote an essay called "Politics" and then an essay called "Experience," in which he tried to come to terms with human limitations. His faith returned, but it was in tension with experience. Stephen E. Whicher writes, "Only as we sense this tension of faith and experience in him can we catch the quality of his affirmation" (43). During the Civil War, Whitman became deeply involved with visiting the wounded in the Washington, D.C. hospitals where he became a volunteer nurse. The following lines are from his 1865 poem "The Wound-Dresser" (and these lines are inscribed in concrete at Washington's Dupont Circle Metro station):

> Thus in silence in dreams' projections,
> Returning, resuming, I thread my way through the hospitals,
> The hurt and wounded I pacify with soothing hand,
> I sit by the restless all the dark night, some are so young,
> Some suffer so much, I recall the experience sweet and sad. . . . (311)

I want students to see that experience hugely affected earlier writers, and was as much on their minds as it is for us.

In autobiography, experience is important for the writer and the reader. It's worth exploring what experience means. In *Reading Autobiography: A Guide for Interpreting Life Narratives*, Sidonie Smith and Julia Watson write that "It is important to theorize what we call experience because the narrator's lived experience is the primary kind of evidence asserted in autobiographical acts . . ." (33). This theorizing of experience problematizes the term and gives us an entryway for discussing an autobiography. Smith and Watson distinguish between events (the things that happen to us, the material events of our lives) and the meaning of those events, which they define as experience. They write that "we make that meaning, or the 'experience' of those events, discursively, in language and as narrative" (32). They also argue that experience is socially constructed and "the authority of experience" is not a fixed entity. In some narratives experience lacks legitimacy and authority; "in other narratives the authority to narrate is hard-won in a constant engagement with readers posited as skeptical unbelieving, resistant, and even hostile. Thus the instability of something called the authority of experience suggests how the category of experience itself is socially, culturally, historically, and politically negotiated" (34). They quote Joan W. Scott in *Feminists Theorize the Political:* "This thing called experience is at once always already an interpretation *and* is in need of interpretation" (37). Woolman and Gandhi would argue for "Truth" that is outside of human subjective judgment, but they might agree that our understanding of it "is in need of interpretation." Quakerism, like other faiths, is a social construct defined by community and interpreted by the community and the individual. Our social context shapes how we interpret the experience. Reading creates layers of interpretation.

I am drawn to recent descriptions of what seems a larger understanding of inward experience, joining mystical knowing and quantum physics. Our inward experience of knowing, it has been argued, is evidence of our participation in the unfolding universe. Coelho writes that numinous experiences reflect what we are learning from quantum physics of "the nonvisible interiority of matter"; she writes that "The base of the universe seethes with creativity" (4, 5). In the early twentieth century, scientists described the atom as 99.99% empty space. Now, scientists are redefining that "emptiness" as a "plenum" – "a seeming emptiness that is actually full" (5). My first experience of Quaker worship, and my understanding since then of what happens inwardly during the meditation of silent worship, resonates with the inward "seething energy" that others describe. Thomas Kelly, in *A Testament of Devotion*, writes about the "subterranean sanctuary of the soul, where Light never fades, but burns, a perpetual Flame, where the wells of living water of divine revelation rise up continuously, day by day, and hour by hour, steady and transfiguring" (31). Anne Hillman describes a spiritual experience in meditation this way: "Suddenly, something in you – not sense nor sight nor sound nor smell but some other faculty – beholds a vast and boiling ocean that pours itself in the room / into you and leaves you streaming with energy" (qtd. in Coelho 15). Although I couldn't have verbalized it at the time, this sense of energy within is the feeling of liberation I experienced at my first Quaker Meeting. We are aware of the universe without us and within us. To say that experience is contextual and interpreted does not seem to me to exclude any of these ways of understanding experience.

As with the Tao, we have a sense of something larger than any name we can give it. The early Quakers called it Truth, and they were Seekers after Truth, a name which for them encompassed all. Quakers use the phrase "the way opens" to express a mystical sense of directionality that we sense as inward leadings, that Coelho argues may resonate with the directionality of a birthing, unfolding universe. As I think about nonviolence in this realm, I think of it as honoring our place in that universe in which "the way opens." Violence (whether war, physical violence to the individual, oppression, or verbal violence) is that which stops one from experiencing this energy; violence is that which prevents a person from taking part in the way opening.

This Speaks to My Condition

Earlier in my career as a teacher, I would hear students respond to a book by saying, "I can relate to this" or even the odd statement "This is relatable." I tried to steer them away from this response. Now I see that "I can relate to this" can be the beginning of an important statement. It expresses a good impulse, which can lead to more articulate comments that one expects from experienced readers. We are looking for ways to connect to a text and for how it speaks to the needs, interests, and issues in our lives. When George Fox wrote of his discovery that "There is one, even Christ Jesus, that can speak to thy condition" (11), he expressed the ideal of looking to one's Inward Teacher. He also gave Quakers a phrase, "This speaks to my condition," which expresses the meaningfulness of a Friend's spoken ministry. It seems to me that this is often how we read as well, particularly spiritual autobiography.

We are energized and awakened by the opportunity to talk about what speaks to us. Day's *The Long Loneliness* and Edelman's *Lanterns* reached the students sometimes on a personal level. One student, Daniel, wrote about his current doubts and his need for validation:

> As I began reading *The Long Loneliness*, the autobiography of celebrated Catholic activist Dorothy Day, I found that the problems I face today are not unique and that my own indecision and doubt do not bar me from living a valuable life. . . . The past three months have proved difficult, as I grapple with decisions that seem as though they will have far reaching, possibly permanent, effects on my life. . . . I have also been affected negatively by the harmful habit of comparing myself, along with my goals, aversions, and preferences, to those of others.

In this passage, Daniel realizes from reading Day's book that his "own indecision and doubt do not bar" him "from living a valuable life." In his last Small Writing for the class, Daniel wrote about a similar soul searching and validation. This time it was about how he and his father communicate with each other, not so much through words as working together repairing fences on their property:

"I was lucky," my father always tells me. . . . I do not disagree. He's outdriven the Highway Patrol, survived nicotine poisoning while curing tobacco as a summer job, and, when I was four, he came close to crushing me with a tractor. . . . he's lucky as Hell. But my father is done with luck now, and he doesn't want his children to be lucky like he was, either. He wants us to be prepared. But I don't know if that's what I want. Good stories don't come from being prepared. They come from the short-cuts, the improvisations, the split-second decisions. They come from luck. And I think I'd like to be lucky, too. But I can't tell my father this. I can only nod my head and validate his warnings. . . . The two of us, each silent and unknown to the other, holding out for that moment which might bring us together for all time. It may never come, but that doesn't mean anything to us. We have to remain. Desperados waiting for a train.

Here Daniel is doing what I believe our class is so much about – that is, thinking about relationships and what matters here. When I read pieces like this, I am pleased to see my students taking ownership for and valuing their experience. This might seem like a simple idea, but it has large implications for how students—or anyone—can be empowered in their lives.

Often in our Small Writings students shared with the class things not directly related to the autobiographical texts. Sometimes these took on elements of confession (which we talked about, too, as so important to the history of spiritual autobiography). Often they spoke of the therapeutic value of doing this writing. "The past few years have been interesting," Kelsey wrote in one piece about her current situation. "I cried often and alone and drank myself numb most nights, yet maintained fair grades and worked my ass off. . . . But I remind myself that it's not for me, I'm getting this degree and learning these things and working my butt off for the kids of the future." In a second writing a few weeks later, she wrote about her awakening and shocking experience in a travel course to Ghana, where she saw malnourished children and mothers. She visited a castle, which was built by Europeans and once held thousands of people crowded into filthy dungeons before they were shipped west and sold into slavery. She writes, "I dropped to my knees, and sobbed." And in a third writing, several weeks later, she spoke about her work with inner-city children at Roanoke's West End Center:

I tell you of these children, because they are the exact reason for why I wanted to dedicate my life to helping others. The violence, abuse, brokenness, is something no child should ever have to go through. I vowed that I would make a difference for these kids. And yet I sit in my classes, and have a prepared answer for what I want to do with my life when people ask. I always say that I want to be a school counselor for inner city children, and implement peace and non-violence programs into high school curriculum. Doesn't sound too shabby, right? I've been thinking a lot about what that actually means though. It's easy to talk about wanting to make change. . . .

I feel privileged to read writings like Kelsey's. The progression in these three writings is remarkable. Although she doesn't mention our course texts, her honesty about the struggles of finding her own path in the world is similar to what we encountered in each of the spiritual autobiographies.

The Quaker form of worship is not only about the individual but it also has implications for community. It is important that Friends do this together. Similarly, it is important that we did what we did in class together. Responding to these autobiographies together, we speak to each other in statements from our own lives. Our discussions and writing grow out of where our lives meet the text and the world.

Each of the autobiographies addresses issues about the individual and the community. In the class, we talked about various aspects of individualism, including aspects of feminism and masculinity, and various aspects of living in community. Each of the spiritual autobiographies that we read says a great deal about the connections between community and the individual's discovery of vocation. In *The Long Loneliness*, Day provides guidance, which can be applied to nonviolent movements: quoting St. John of the Cross, she says, "Where there is no love, put love, and you will find love." In the realm of social justice movements, this advice teaches an activist to apply, through one's inward life and outward action, what one cannot find in the world, and it will be returned. In *Lanterns*, Edelman describes how she was adrift and angry in the Jim Crow South. She discovers purpose in the Civil Rights movement. Fueled by her Christian faith, she is able to direct her anger into meaningful action. She becomes the first Black female attorney in Mississippi and later founder of the Children's Defense Fund.

Several students in the class wrote about community and vocation. One young man, Wes, was moved by Edelman's recognition of the saving guidance she had received from others:

> . . . she describes growing up in the Civil Rights Movement, and ultimately becoming a prominent figure in it. Yet in her words she captured the power of community, something that I feel we may have lost as a society. Throughout her writings she is quick to give credit to

others, and to show how she benefited from their tutelage and courage. She extols importance of community, of risk taking, and of courage in the face of adversity. Edelman grew up in a dynamic and classic community, and when she was adrift as a young college student it was the community of the civil rights movement that saved her from despair.

Wes was not only interested in this new vision of community but also in the way that Edelman survived a period of despair in college, after she had returned from study abroad. The community of Spellman College and her involvement in the Civil Rights movement saved her. As Wes writes, "Edelman had her wakeup call at this moment, and she realized that she was an instrumental figure in a larger fight."

I chose Edelman's *Lanterns: A Memoir of Mentors* partly because it is devoted to the mentors who shaped her life and nurtured her through her education and early career. I invited students to reflect on the many people who have been positive influences in their lives: parents, grandparents, aunts, and uncles, but also teachers, coaches, and elders. Wes wrote that "Her parents taught her the importance of helping to serve others at an early age, and because she was raised in such a community setting she was naturally more attuned to the needs and pains of others."

Alejandro, another student, found that Day's *The Long Loneliness* spoke to him about issues of vocation. He was drawn to her writing hardships and struggles, and her need for frequent reaffirmation of purpose. He says, "Day exposes the awareness that life is a constant struggle, a long loneliness in which to cultivate ourselves, our sense of spirituality and purpose, and a commitment to the reaffirmation of those commitments." Day's book contains a passage about a group of young men who talked all night about whether they should register for the draft (71). Alejandro's comment about this passage is a touching expression of the life of the mind. He says, "I entirely believe that those experiences, where young minds come together are where the future begins to come together. Fellowship is important in challenging and cultivating our way of thought, and also our sense of identity." For him the intensity of Day's struggle, and what he calls her "commitment to commitment" is what he found most compelling.

Another student, John, was interested in how Edelman wrote about life's lessons, tests, and consequences. John used a quotation from another writer to introduce his thought:

As Wallace Stegner once put it in his novel, *All the Little Live Things*, "There is a sense in which we are all each other's consequences." The next thing to directly happen from action is the reception of that action through others; effectively, we are the ones who shape ourselves. By instructing myself to be wary of the consequences my actions can bring, I'm more aware of the good that can be done.

John took from reading Edelman's memoir that he could consider how the consequences of his actions could help him direct his efforts toward the good.

In each of these student writings, whether responding to an autobiography directly or indirectly, I felt that we were making connections with important ways to think about our own lives. Often class discussion grew out of autobiographical passages where the writers look back on their younger selves struggling with moral choices. Woolman writes about an early experience of cruelty toward animals, his disobedience to his mother, but also later as a young man working in a dry-goods store writing a bill of sale for an enslaved woman, because his employer's request caught him off guard. Day writes about her decision to have an abortion, later to have a child without being married, and gradually to accept a devout life of faith in the Catholic Church. In class we examined how such situations shape these writers' future direction as well as how they learn from looking back on their lives.

David Brooks argues in *The Road to Character* that young people today need to learn how to think about moral decisions. He cites a study done at Notre Dame University in which students couldn't describe a moral problem: "Their default position was that moral choices are just a question of what feels right inside, whether it arouses a comfortable emotion" (258), and thus each person's opinion must be right. As Brooks writes, "They didn't understand that a moral dilemma arises when two legitimate moral values clash" (258). The autobiographies present us with such moral dilemmas.

I also wanted us to consider the implications of the writers' omissions. Readers want Woolman to tell us how he and Sarah Ellis came to be married, what their life together was like, and even what he said in his confrontations with those with whom he disagreed. But those do not fall within his purpose of telling how he felt the Spirit of God had acted in his life. Gandhi tells us, in his Introduction, that a friend had advised him not to write an autobiography, because "Writing an autobiography is a practice peculiar to the West" (vii). This gives Gandhi pause. He explains that "it is not my purpose to attempt a real autobiography. I simply want to tell the story of my numerous experiments with truth," but he says he will omit most of "My experiments in the political field" because these are already well known (vii-viii). For many of us, we need and want to hear more about his work in the political field. In Dorothy Day's case, she chooses not to include painful details from her early adult life such as a disastrous love affair with Lionel Moise, who was a newspaper man she met working at a hospital and who convinced her to have an abortion, and her agreeing to marry Berkeley Tobey, a man twice her age (Brooks 80). Considering the things left out problematized the reading for us, as we discussed each writer's purpose, but also as we thought about what we would omit from our own autobiographical writing. The decision to leave things out is also a kind of agency.

What Canst Thou Say?

The idea of individuals being empowered to speak was of great importance to the early Quaker movement. Speaking came to have large implications for taking action based upon principle. When students are given opportunities to speak in class they are discovering what they have to say, finding their voice, and realizing that they can make a difference.

Early Friends objected to university-trained priests, whom they saw as corrupt and uninspired. Geoffrey Nuttall, in his Introduction to George Fox's *Journal*, writes that Fox's experience had a distinctive message of inclusiveness:

> With the recovery of the Bible in the vernacular, Christians had come to hear the voice of God speaking not only to the prophets and apostles of old but through these to themselves. The word of the Lord endureth for ever, and what was written in Scripture was found to possess contemporary significance and power, and to provide a message which could be preached to others with conviction. 'You will say, Christ saith this, and the apostles say this; but what canst thou say?' . . . He urged men to attend to the words of the Spirit within their hearts . . . (xxiv).

"The Spirit within their hearts" would be referred to later as the "Inward Teacher." By trusting the inward teacher, Fox and others discovered a new understanding of authority. Friends believed there was "that of God in every person," which meant that women as well as men could speak in worship – an idea that was both democratic and liberating. I want students to feel empowered, too, and to respond assertively to the question "what canst thou say?"

Turning to one's inward teacher to find direction became a pattern linking worship to action. Woolman's *Journal* is well known for its expression of this pattern of moral action as both an inward and outward motion. William A.

Christian, Sr., argues, in an article called "Inwardness and Outward Concerns: A Study of John Woolman's Thought," that there is no contradiction between inwardness and action, but rather a dynamic relationship. Woolman turned inward to listen for the leadings of the Spirit from which he was guided to act upon his social concerns. Inward devotion does not always generate action in the world, Christian writes, but Woolman turned inward to find "an inward principle," which created an unusual sensitivity to the suffering of people and animals. "Woolman does not identify the inward principle with God," Christian writes. "It 'proceeds from' God. God's love for man 'begets' man's love for man" (99). William Penn says, in *No Cross, No Crown*, "True Godliness does not turn men out of the world, but enables them to live better in it, and excites their endeavours to mend it" (qtd. in Christian 95). Over several decades in response to inward leadings, Woolman felt led to take more and more self-denying actions, which included giving up his lucrative dry goods business in order to have more time for his ministry and antislavery efforts, refusing to wear dyed clothing because of the oppressive methods of creating the dyes, walking rather than traveling on horseback so that he might identify with the slaves, refusing to send letters through the post because of the cruel treatment of horses and children on the coaches, and giving up use of silver utensils because of the cruel conditions of the mines. He worked with a small group of reformers to end slave owning among Friends and through war-tax refusal to avoid complicity in the French and Indian War. Through such actions as well as reaching others through writing, Woolman became a precursor to the great nonviolent activists of the twentieth century. As he took on each additional task, he was acting upon a sense of duty that was inseparable from his inward spiritual life.

Probably the most famous moment in Gandhi's *Autobiography* also involves the realization of one's duty. Gandhi describes the scene where, as a young attorney newly arrived in South Africa, he is kicked off a train for sitting in a whites-only car. His moral dilemma becomes a turning point in his life and in the *Autobiography*. He spends the night in the cold train station first thinking that he does not have to take this abuse and should go back to India. But then he begins to realize what he is called to do. "I began to think of my duty," Gandhi writes. "Should I fight for my rights or go back to India?" (97). In that long night alone, he comes to the realization that he "should try, if possible, to root out the disease and suffer hardships in the process . . . . So I decided to take the next available train to Pretoria" (97). Here was the moment when he found his vocation. In our class, we talked about his understanding of "duty" – a term which I find especially challenging because of my West Point and Army experience. Gandhi and Woolman both bring a new understanding to the term for me.

Parker Palmer's book, *Let Your Life Speak*, explores how the ideal of "what canst thou say" evolved in his own understanding. He writes, "I ran across the old Quaker saying, 'Let your life speak.' I found those words encouraging, and I thought I understood what they meant: 'Let the highest truths and values guide you. Live up to those demanding standards in everything you do'" (2). He goes on to say that this "youthful understanding" gradually transformed from "a simplistic brand of moralism" to a more mature understanding of vocation. "Vocation does not come from willfulness," he writes, but from listening. "I must listen to my life and try to understand what it is truly about" (3-4). Autobiographies are about lives speaking. When we take actions to make our communities or the world more peaceful and just, we are also letting our lives speak.

Palmer also wrote in an essay, "The Meeting for Learning," about a concept of education that is based upon this idea of turning inward. He based the essay on his experience as a teacher and dean of students at Pendle Hill. One of the key themes he considers is the idea of expectation. He writes of "the expectation that, if we give it space and time, truth will come to us" (2). He was intrigued and moved by how the Quaker worship modeled "a meeting for learning" partially through a "democracy of knowledge" because there is a trust in what will emerge from the group. In the classroom, the teacher's role is not just intellectual, but rather "to nurture and encourage the expertise of others . . . what must finally be trusted in a meeting for learning is not a text or the group or the technique of the teacher, but a truth that lies beyond all our devises" (4). Expectation and trust go hand in hand as we look to our inward lives for how we respond. Quakers talk about "expectant waiting" in the Meeting for worship – an idea that translates to reading literature and to writing. It involves the small "f" faith or trust that if we have the expectation that good things will come to us, either from the text or from within ourselves to speak or write, the way will open. We will find what we can say.

In our class we discussed the motion of going inward to find one's outward direction. Students were interested in how we can be effective working in the world to reduce violence and injustice. One student, Rachel, wrote about the ways in which Woolman and Gandhi both increased their effectiveness by not making others their enemies. She admired Woolman for not verbally attacking slave owners and quotes him saying how he "went alone to the houses, and, in fear of the Lord, acquainted them with the exercise I was under; and thus, sometimes by a few words, I found myself discharged from a heavy burden" (Woolman's *Journal*, Moulton edition 97). Rachel says, "Because of Woolman's choice to act peacefully, he as one man affected better change than he would have done if he had attacked these people head on." Rachel felt that Gandhi's self-sacrifice "even for those who oppressed him and his people, was the main quality that set him apart as a leader with the potential to create the enormous amounts of change." She was intrigued by Gandhi's Christ-like behavior: "Love for one's enemy is a principle often attributed to the Christian religion. . . . Walter Wink, a Biblical scholar, wrote in *Grasping Gandhi* that 'Nonviolence is not a peripheral concern but the very heart of Christ's message' (Cortright 13)." Rachel was interested in how Christians have failed to follow this teaching, and yet Gandhi, a Hindu, embraced the teaching of the Sermon on the Mount.

Another student, Kayleigh, was drawn to Gandhi's Hindu universalism and his acceptance of other religions. She writes that "Gandhi once said: 'The essence of all religions is one. Only their approaches are different' (Rao)." She expressed her concern about how religious conflicts have been behind many of our wars, and she admired Gandhi because "He spent much of his life trying to help others seek an acceptance of other religions for the possibility that it would lead to a greater understanding between individuals and cultures." She too saw this acceptance of others growing out of his upbringing,

> . . . because of his father's role in exposing him to other religions which added to his education on truth and acceptance: [in Gandhi's words] "He had, besides, Musalman and Parsi friends, who would talk to him about their own faiths, and he would listen to them always with respect, and often with interest" (*Autobiography* 29). Gandhi's father did not force his own ideologies upon him, but familiarized him with different beliefs. Because of this, throughout his education, Gandhi assumed responsibility of completely understanding how and why people believe in the things they do so that he could better empathize with them and the struggles they faced.

In her reading of Gandhi's *Autobiography*, Kayleigh was thinking about the timely issues of interfaith literacy, acceptance, and understanding.

For a long time, I've felt that, in a course or a curriculum, "coverage of material" is a less important goal than the quality of the students' experience. Experience includes the way students are engaged with the material. One way we can accomplish this is to help students return to the personal essay, an approach advocated by G. Douglas Atkins in *Estranging the Familiar: Toward a Revitalized Critical Writing*. He writes of the essay's "capaciousness and artistic possibilities, wonders and delights perhaps never more apparent than now" (ix). "When the essay combines good writing with the concerns of the personal, . . . it becomes a form of criticism that is readable, vital, and potentially attractive to a large readership, . . . despite claims to the contrary there is no inherent incompatibility between the essay and modern theory" (back cover). In a similar impulse that values a more holistic approach to education, teachers and educational theorists are questioning the effectiveness of over reliance upon lecturing, as opposed to more engaging techniques. Annie Murphy Paul, in "Are College Lectures Unfair?", looks at recent claims that the college lecture might be "biased against undergraduates who are not white, male and affluent?" While I try to use brief talks by me to set up a discussion or to share a bit of useful information from my own expertise, I want students to be challenged to engage actively with the material. I noticed an unusual kind of listening at Pendle Hill when I experienced classes there, and I have heard others comment on this. When people speak from their own experience, others tend to listen, and when people listen deeply, those speaking tend to say extraordinary things. But this takes practice. We must help our students learn to listen.

There are multiple ways we can read texts like these four autobiographies. I have chosen a way of reading that attempts to mirror a holistic approach that borrows from Quaker ideals: letting the texts speak to the fullness of students' lives, not exclusively their intellects or, on the flip side, primarily their feelings. Reading Woolman, Gandhi, Day, and Edelman, we see how, as agents of nonviolent social change, they are models for living and acting in the world. My aspiration is for the students to be empowered as readers by valuing their own experience with these autobiographies and in their own lives. I want the reading experience to be a kind of liberation, where we discover what we can say and how we can let our lives speak.

✳ Works Cited ✳

Atkins, G. Douglas. *Estranging the Familiar: Toward a Revitalized Critical Writing.* Athens, GA: The University of Georgia Press, 1992. Print.

Brooks, David. *The Road to Character.* New York: Random House, 2015. Print.

Christian, William A., Sr. "Inwardness and Outward Concerns: A Study of John Woolman's Thought." *Quaker History* 67 (1978): 88-104. Print.

Coelho, Mary Conrow. *Recovering Sacred Presence in a Disenchanted World.* Wallingford, PA: Pendle Hill Publications, 2015. Print.

Compton, Jessica, Wes Knowles, Rachel Miles, Kayleigh Murphy, Daniel Osborne, and Kelsey Reedy. Unpublished papers from our course

"Nonviolence as a Spiritual Journey." Roanoke College, Fall 2014. Print.

Cortright, David. *Gandhi and Beyond: Nonviolence for a New Political Age.* 2nd ed. Boulder, CO: Paradigm, 2009. Print.

Day, Dorothy. *The Long Loneliness.* 1952. New York: HarperCollins, 1997. Print.

Edelman, Marian Wright. *Lanterns: A Memoir of Mentors.* New York: HarperCollins, 1999. Print.

Emerson, Ralph Waldo. "The Poet." *Selections from Ralph Waldo Emerson: An Organic Anthology.* Ed. Stephen E. Whicher. Boston: Houghton Mifflin, 1957. 222-41. Print.

Fox, George. *The Journal of George Fox.* Ed. John L. Nickalls. 1952. London: Religious Society of Friends, 1986. Print.

Gandhi, Mohandas K. *Autobiography: The Story of My Experiments with Truth.* Trans. Mahadev Desai. 1927, 1929. New York: Dover, 1983. Print.

Heller, Mike. "From West Point to Quakerism." Pendle Hill Pamphlet 389. Wallingford, PA: Pendle Hill Publications, April 2007. Print.

---. "'Wait to Be Gathered': The Classroom as Spiritual Place." *Minding the Light: Essays in Friendly Pedagogy.* Eds. Anne Dalke and Barbara Dixson. NY: Peter Lang, 2004. 43-63. Print.

Heller, William E., 1st Lt., to Lt. Col. John T. Burns, Casualty Branch, War Department, Washington DC. 27 Nov. 1945. Copy given to me by my father.

---. Letter to Bryan Sherman. 9 June 2001. Copy given to me by my father.

Kelly, Thomas. *A Testament of Devotion.* NY: Harper and Row, 1941. Print.

O'Reilley, Mary Rose. *Radical Presence: Teaching as Contemplative Practice.* Portsmouth, NH: Boynton/Cook, 1993. Print.

Palmer, Parker. *Let Your Life Speak: Listening for the Voice of Vocation.* San Francisco: Jossey-Bass, 2000. Print.

---. "Meeting for Learning: Education in a Quaker Context." *The Pendle Hill Bulletin.* Wallingford, PA: Pendle Hill, 1976. Print.

Paul, Annie Murphy. "Are College Lectures Unfair?" *The New York Times.* Sunday Review. Web. Sep 12, 2015.

Penington, Isaac. "Some Directions to the Panting Soul." 1661. Glenside, PA: Quaker Heritage Press. Web. 31 Aug. 2015.

Rao, M.S. "Religion and Love to Achieve World Peace." *UN Post.* UN Post, 11 Oct. 2013. Web. 27 Oct. 2014.

Smith, Sidonie, and Julia Watson. *Reading Autobiography: A Guide for Interpreting Life Narratives.* Minneapolis: University of Minnesota Press, 2010. Print.

Whicher, Stephen E. "Emerson's Tragic Sense." *Emerson: A Collection of Critical Essays.* Eds. Milton R. Konvitz and Stephen E. Whicher. Englewood Cliffs, NJ: Prentice-Hall, 1962. 39-45. Print.

Whitman, Walt. "Song of Myself" and "The Wound-Dresser." *Leaves of Grass.* Eds. Sculley Bradley and Harold W. Blodgett. NY: Norton, 1973. 28-89, 308-11. Print.

Woolman, John. *John Woolman: A Nonviolence and Social Change Source Book.* 2nd ed. Eds. Sterling Olmsted and Mike Heller. Wilmington, OH, and Richmond, IN: Wilmington College Peace Resource Center and Friends United Press, 2013. Print.

---. *The Journal and Major Essays of John Woolman.* Ed. Phillips P. Moulton. 1971. Richmond, IN: Friends United Press, 1989. Print.

✳ An Afterword, With Questions ✳

In the January 1999 volume of *PMLA*, Lawrence Buell reported that ethical inquiry had "gained new resonance in literary studies" that might come to rival the paradigmatic dominance of textuality in the 1970s and historicism in the 1980s (7). It was a fascinating and understandable claim, given the number of prominent studies of the literature/ethics nexus that had appeared in the years leading up to the close of the second millennium. The fact that many more studies in this vein arrived in the years following Buell's pronouncement demonstrates the degree of his prescience.[1] Given the consistent emphasis in the essays of this volume on literature's relationship to prophetic vision, spiritual and personal development, and the improvement of social relations and structures (including pacifism and utopian community), we might readily view this book as yet another participant in the broader return to ethical inquiry in literary study. But like literary scholars' engagements with textuality and historicism that we can now see as revisions of earlier paradigms—the New Criticism and the so-called "old historicism" of the nineteenth century, respectively—the "turn to ethics" in literary scholarship could be seen as another such re-turn, taking up with new critical eyes a formerly less-nuanced understanding of the place of literature in social development and society as a whole (think Matthew Arnold's *Culture and Anarchy*).

What seems clearest, both in this volume and in earlier commentary on the topic, is that Quaker engagement with literature, in all its various forms, has always turned towards the ethical. Quakers writing about writing have been concerned primarily with the power of texts to shape human lives, both in

---

[1] Examples of general studies and essay collections include Booth; Garber, Hanssen, and Walkowitz; Rorty; George; and Nussbaum. There are many other recent examples of more specific studies, of which Miller's 2009 investigation of Victorian literature serves as but one instance.

potentially efficacious and debilitating ways. Although Fox's, Barclay's, Penn's, and others' prohibitions against the problems of representation and the dangers of the theater may now strike us as quaint or even misguided, the essays in this volume clearly demonstrate that contemporary Friends valuably express some of the traits of that early Quaker literary-critical DNA, at least insofar as we evince a serious bent towards locating where disciplined spiritual growth and practical engagement for social change might come through encounters with imaginative literature. The focused thoughtfulness, the integrity, with which these essays meet the challenges of interpretation is, furthermore, in its very nature, an expression of the ethical, at least in the classical rhetorical sense of *ethos*. These essays' attention to serious matters in an open and right-ordered fashion bespeaks a depth of character we may rightly celebrate. They show that, rather than simply following the fashion of the day, the Quaker relationship with literary productions has remained steadfastly consistent. "How does this text speak to thy condition?" we have always asked, and we will continue to do so.

As you ponder the ideas and interpretations presented in this book, the following discussion questions may provide opportunities for further thought and reflection:

1. Is there a particularly Quaker approach to the teaching of literature? Would such an approach lead more naturally to ethical inquiry than other approaches? If so, why?
2. Stories, various essays in the collection remind us, can have powerful influences on our lives. By what specific mechanisms does this happen? What particular stories—fictional or non-fictional—have shaped your own life profoundly?
3. In what ways does it make sense to classify spiritual autobiographies, Quaker journals, and memoirs as "literature"? Does that broaden our definition of "literature" too far?
4. Are there any particular features of Quakerism that might have drawn Quaker writers toward science fiction as a genre?
5. Are Quakers sometimes too prone to what Diane Reynolds calls "the backward gaze," a desire to celebrate our peculiarity in ways that can lead to fiction treating Quakerism as a quaint in-group instead of engaging with more substantive matters?
6. How might we write Quaker fiction that does not dwell on peculiarity or quaintness?

7. At a time when humanistic study in colleges and universities seems to be viewed as less and less valuable, how might a Quaker approach to teaching literature demonstrate more clearly the importance of studying this vital human endeavor?
8. How might a Quaker approach to teaching and learning highlight, even in the context of a secular institution, the importance of spiritual inquiry and discovery?

✳ Works Cited ✳

Arnold, Matthew. *Culture and Anarchy*. New Haven: Yale UP, 1994. Print.

Booth, Wayne C. *The Company We Keep: An Ethics of Fiction*. Berkeley: U of California, 1988. Print.

Buell, Lawrence. "Introduction: In Pursuit of Ethics." *PMLA* 114.1 (Jan. 1999): 7-19. Print.

Garber, Marjorie, Beatrice Hanssen, and Rebecca L. Walkowitz, eds. *The Turn to Ethics*. New York and London: Routledge, 2000. Print.

George, Stephen K., ed. *Ethics, Literature, & Theory: An Introductory Reader*. 2nd ed. Lanham, Md.: Rowman & Littlefield, 2005. Print.

Miller, Andrew H. *The Burdens of Perfection: On Ethics and Reading in Nineteenth-Century British Literature*. Ithaca and London: Cornell UP, 2008. Print.

Nussbaum, Martha Craven. *The Fragility of Goodness: Luck and Ethics in Greek Tragedy and Philosophy*. Cambridge and New York: Cambridge UP, 1986. Print.

Rorty, Richard. *Contingency, Irony, and Solidarity*. Cambridge and New York: Cambridge UP. 1989. Print.

Printed in Great Britain
by Amazon